Coaching in Mental Health Service Settings and Beyond

T0349993

Coaching in Mental Health Service Settings and Beyond

Practical Applications

Jenny Forge

 Open University Press

Open University Press
McGraw-Hill Education
8th Floor, 338 Euston Road
London
England
NW1 3BH

email: enquiries@openup.co.uk
world wide web: www.openup.co.uk

and Two Penn Plaza, New York, NY 10121-2289, USA

First edition published 2022

A catalogue record of this book is available from the British Library

Commissioning Editor: Eleanor Christie
Editorial Assistant: Zoe Osman
Content Product Manager: Ali Davis
Head of Portfolio Marketing: Bryony Waters

ISBN-13: 9780335250479
ISBN-10: 0335250475
eISBN: 9780335250486

Library of Congress Cataloging-in-Publication Data
CIP data applied for

Typeset by Transforma Pvt. Ltd., Chennai, India

Praise page

"This book elegantly and systematically describes both the principles and practice of coaching, with a special emphasis on work in mental health services. Dr Forge manages to draw on a wide variety of established, relevant and useful theory whilst maintaining a focus on the distinctiveness of the coaching approach. In practical terms, the case studies are of real value in illustrating what 'good looks like' in coaching in this context. I believe this book will be valuable in supporting practitioners in improving their personal effectiveness as organisational leaders, supervisors, managers or clinicians at a time when our services are facing unprecedented staffing challenges."

Paul Tiffin, *Professor of Health Services and*
Workforce Research, University of York, UK

"This is an excellent book about the use of coaching to support mental health. The author skilfully walks the reader through basic and advanced coaching skills, using multiple case studies to demonstrate how coaching models, in particular the CLEAR model, are applied in practice. The learning is deepened through the use of reflective questions. As the title suggest, the book has direct relevance for multidisciplinary healthcare workers looking to support mental health recovery, but also wider applications to anyone struggling with mental health or trauma-related challenges, and to culture change in mental health settings. I thoroughly recommend it."

Mike Slade, *Professor of Mental Health Recovery and*
Social Inclusion, University of Nottingham, UK

"This book is a very useful work for any Mental Health Professional with an interest in Coaching, whether as a Coach or Coachee. The author has written with impressive clarity, and the content unfolds throughout the book, moving from the theoretical and ethical underpinnings to the use and value of coaching in Mental Health settings, both clinical and professional. Case studies and personal experience are used to highlight specific points. I recommend it highly."

Russell Hodgson, *Mental Health Nurse and MBCT Teacher*

"Written in an engaging style, this excellent book is full of practical techniques including powerful coaching questions as well as useful suggestions. It is vividly illustrated with relevant examples and memorable, amusing analogies. Like a good map, it reveals the best routes to successful coaching whilst also indicating potential obstacles and how to avoid them. As well as heartily recommending it to participants

on our coaching courses it is also a perfect guide to having coaching conversations with colleagues, patients and carers. I believe this innovative book will contribute to further developing a beneficial coaching culture within mental health services."

Dr Simon Michaelson, Consultant Psychiatrist and
Coaching Course Facilitator

"Jenny Forge draws on her two careers as a psychiatrist and coach, together with her personal journey, to offer us a practical and realistic guide to coaching in mental health settings. I so enjoyed her refreshing approach as a sceptic of slavish adherence to models and theories. This is both a compelling read, and a deeply serious book. She makes a confident and persuasive argument for a coaching approach in helping mental health service users and staff alike. I expect it to reach essential reading status for all mental health practitioners in short order."

Joe Reilly, NHS Workplace Mediator and Visiting
Professor, University of York, UK

For Sylvia and Frank

Contents

Acknowledgements

I would like to start by thanking all the people who have joined me for coaching conversations in a range of contexts. I am very fortunate to have shared those conversations. On my coaching journey, I have valued the company of many colleagues, coaches and friends. I'm sorry that there is not space to name you all here.

I am thankful especially to Peronel Barnes, Andy Gilbert, Delia Lloyd, Simon Michaelson, Wendy Minhinnett, Claire Pedrick and Mike Slade. In addition, Rob Briner, Windy Dryden, Errol Green, Adrian Furnham, Arti Maini, Kath Roberts, Julie Steel, Katharine St. John-Brooks and the team at McGraw-Hill have been generous in giving me time and opportunity to learn from them. And I'll close by expressing love and appreciation for my family: Paul, Kate and Ruth.

Part 1

Setting the Scene

Introduction to Part 1

'Where am I heading next?', 'How will I get there?' and, come to think of it, 'Do I really want to go?' Throughout our lives, we ask ourselves these kinds of metaphorical questions. The thinking that we do in response to them, and the answers we come up with, can greatly affect what we gain from, and give to, the world. In relation to such questions, coaching has a place in helping us to move forward.

In the coming chapters, I describe what I mean by coaching and show how it has an important part to play in the sphere of mental health care. Good coaching is about having constructive and productive conversations that spark people to make the most of their personal and professional potential. Coaching is no magic bullet, but it has value. I argue that coaching:

- can contribute directly to better mental health care, by the appropriate use of coaching approaches with service users and families/carers;
- can also improve the functioning of the organizations that provide that care, by the use of coaching approaches within the workforce.

To support the claim of a role for coaching, the book highlights the utility of coaching models, particularly CLEAR (Hawkins and Smith, 2013). When used properly and at the right time, I show how such models can provide valuable shape and coherence to a range of important conversations in the context of mental health care provision. The primary focus of this book is on one-to-one coaching, but many of the principles and interventions can also be applied in group or team settings.

Coaching approaches can be valuable in supporting people using mental health services to develop their resourcefulness, self-compassion and connection with what matters to them. Also, for people working in the organizations that provide mental health care, I suggest that coaching can promote their abilities to do important jobs proficiently and aid their well-being.

1 Some context

Introduction

In the twenty-first century, it seems, coaches are everywhere we look. There are coaches employed to help people with their careers, with their multi-million businesses and with their sock drawers. However, the coaching boom of recent years has been met with some scepticism. In a world brimming with all kinds of coaching, the term risks a lack of meaning. Some people hold a misperception that coaches just sit around having expensive, cosy chats. This view can paint a picture of coaches as ineffectual charlatans. 'Just another human accessory for people with more money than friends' (Dowling, 2006), was one characterization of the role of coach in an article in *The Guardian* newspaper.

While I understand how such scepticism may have arisen, I assert that coaching can have real meaning and value. Coaching can facilitate worthwhile understanding and change. And that process is often far from cosy!

This chapter unfolds as follows. The first section engages with the meteoric rise of coaching in recent years. Although I am sympathetic to some of the critics of the coaching *Zeitgeist*, the main problem concerns the proper governance of those calling themselves professional coaches, rather than coaching itself. Coaches who 'over-sell' coaching as an answer to almost all predicaments turn people right off it.

I then move on to consider an overview of some of the concepts that inform how coaching is used. In particular, ideas and theories rooted in applied behavioural and psychological science help us to understand the potential effectiveness of coaching.

Finally, I discuss the vital role that coaching approaches can play in the mental health care field, and briefly introduce the CLEAR model. The chapter closes with an overview of the book.

Coaching: boom and bust?

Think of almost anything you want to do in this day and age, and you can probably find a coach claiming they will help you do it better. The coaching sector is wide ranging and, arguably, still relatively ungoverned. This means that the number of coaches (self-identified or possessing various coaching qualifications) and the full extent of the industry is hard to quantify in an accurate way.

According to the International Coaching Federation Global Coaching Study 2020 (ICF, 2020), there were an estimated 71,000 trained professional coach practitioners worldwide in 2019. This was an increase of 33 per cent on the 2015 estimate, while in 2009 the figure was 47,500. And there are many more other people who advertise themselves as coaches.

Rob Briner, Professor of Organizational Psychology at Queen Mary University of London, once expressed his sense of 'never [being] more than six feet away from a coach' (Briner, 2012: 4). He had a point, and this comment is emblematic of a backlash of sorts against certain aspects of coaching.

I became interested in professional coaching some years ago and at first had more than a few reservations myself. It had a 'Wild West' feel, with a lack of standardization or order. I knew that some so-called professional coaches with dubious qualifications were making overblown, unfounded claims about coaching, whilst charging hefty sums for their services. These were self-appointed coaching sages. I was not convinced by people who touted near magical powers of coaching. And I thought that if coaching really was such a potent thing, there seemed scant awareness or caution about its potential negative effects. It all seemed a bit too shiny.

But I came to realize that the problem was not essentially with coaching, but rather with the difficulties of regulating such a sprawling field. The surge in coaching was not initially associated with proper governance, and this proper governance is still a work in progress.

Most people can enhance their conversations by learning to use coaching principles, but the title of professional coach requires more. I believe this title should be reserved for those who have received thorough training and have gained supervised experience and accreditation with a professional coaching body.[1] Such bodies include the International Coach Federation (ICF), the European Mentoring and Coaching Council (EMCC) and the Association for Coaching (AC). These organizations have become increasingly well-established and have burgeoning memberships. These institutions provide checks and balances in relation to ethical and effective coaching practice.

Despite some reservations, I wanted to learn more about becoming a professional coach, and believed (as it turned out, correctly) that this would also add something extra to my work as a psychiatrist. My decision to become a coach stemmed, in part, from an unanticipated event in my life that led me to develop new perspectives. I became seriously physically ill and underwent some gruelling treatment before returning to health. During this period, I did a lot of thinking about how I wanted to shape my future life, including my work. I was on the receiving end of health care rather than providing it, and that was an interesting situation for me. In a way, weirdly, it was a liberating time, and I decided to train as a coach as well as continuing to work as a doctor.

Coaching involves having enriching conversations, and we all know there is sometimes treasure to be found in good conversations. They can release surprising wisdom and uncover strengths we never knew we had. Such conversations can allow us to develop fresh insights and find new routes forwards. The progress that ensues may take the form of great strides or sometimes just small steps, but even very modest progress counts.

The growth of evidence

There is a growing body of evidence to support the benefits of coaching, and researchers are constantly adding to it. Many of the contributions come from the fields of coaching psychology, positive psychology and organizational psychology.[2]

There is research giving credence to the view that well-being, career satisfaction and goal attainment can be improved with coaching (Grover and Furnham, 2016). In the 2014 book *Mastery in Coaching*, Jonathan Passmore argued that there is conclusive evidence of coaching as a significant tool to support learning, behaviour change and performance improvement. Suzy Green and Stephen Palmer assert that 'Overall, it is clear to see how coaching can be a significant medium in which to support individuals to build resilience ... to reframe challenges and to look for and embrace opportunities' (Green and Palmer, 2019). That is heartening.

There is also evidence for the merit of using coaching approaches in some direct clinical mental health work.[3] The explicit use of coaching methods in the clinical field has grown more popular in recent years as the 'recovery approach' has gained ground. This approach emphasizes partnership between those accessing mental health care and staff, and the value for service users of working towards personally meaningful, self-chosen goals (Bird et al., 2014). These are coaching principles. Coaching skills are an extremely worthwhile addition to a practitioner's repertoire of competencies.

However, the construction of an evidence base for coaching is an ongoing process. There are considerable challenges for those researching the effectiveness of coaching.[4] Coaching may seem as if it is 'working' but whether it is, and what 'working' really means, and for whom, are not straightforward areas of inquiry. If we want to provide coaching that is justified by, and grounded in, evidence, we need to draw on tested theories and models of applied behavioural and psychological science, adult learning, sociology and business management. We will explore this further in Chapter 3 of the book.

Coaching and mental health settings

Coaching is, of course, not a panacea to resolve the complex challenges of shaping and 'delivering' good mental health care. But coaching certainly has something to add.

I have been a doctor for 35 years, and a consultant psychiatrist for 25 years. I am also a qualified professional coach. This experience stands me in good stead to see the role for coaching approaches in the management and operation of mental health services and, importantly, as a part of the care that should be available for those who access those services.

Unfortunately, it is not rare for people who are severely affected by mental illness to be misconstrued and inadequately supported by services and by our communities. At the same time, mental health care and the promotion of emotional well-being is sometimes an over-medicalized area in Western society, and mental illness seems to be talked about more than ever. Coaching approaches that support people to develop their potential and capabilities lend a broader, more holistic emphasis to mental health care.

When mental health practitioners first hear about coaching, it is not that unusual for them to assume that they know how to do it and will be automatically good at it. They are inclined to think that their training and their experience working in mental health care as, for example, a psychologist, nurse, psychiatrist, psychotherapist or social worker means that coaching will be a doddle. I admit to having initially held this kind of assumption myself, and it is certainly true that many mental health practitioners make great coaches, able to draw on ready skills and natural talents. But that does not mean effective coaching is automatically easy for them, or that there is not much to learn and practise.

Throughout the book, I showcase a variety of coaching approaches and methods that, in my experience, have value in the mental health care arena and beyond. I do this within the conversational structure provided by the CLEAR model. Metaphorically, coaching models and frameworks can be seen as containers in which conversations take place, or like the outlines within which coachee and coach can colour together. It is worth emphasizing that to be of real value, coaching models need to be used where rapport has been established and the level of trust is high.

In brief, CLEAR is an acronym where the letters represent five stages of a coaching process. These are:

C = Contract
L = Listen
E = Explore
A = Action
R = Review

The CLEAR model is catchy to remember and logical. That is not to say it is always easy to apply in a conversation. Yet, setting the intention to have a conversation along CLEAR lines can of itself be useful: I have found that even when the structure is followed only loosely, it lends a greater sense of effective flow to the conversation.

A road map for this book

Chapters 1–5 form the first part of the book, 'Setting the Scene'. Following this introductory chapter, Chapter 2 provides fundamental information about coaching, charts the competencies required to do it well and considers coaching in mental health care contexts in a broad-brush way.

In Chapter 3, I show how coaching is both similar to, and different from, related activities such as mentoring or psychological therapy. I sketch out some concepts which underpin effective coaching and highlight the fact that coaches should seek to understand different cultural perspectives in the coaching relationship and process.

Chapter 4 offers food for thought about the significant benefits of using coaching models and frameworks to guide coaching conversations, and I also argue that models have some limitations. Coaching is all about the coachee and being present for the coachee, not all about the model being used or the coach. In Chapter 5, I explore three valuable coaching models.

Part 2 of the book, 'Coaching Conversations with a CLEAR Scaffold', is made up of Chapters 6–11. Throughout these chapters, the focus is on practical suggestions and guidance that will improve coaching knowledge and skills. I describe and elaborate on techniques, questions and attitudes. They are presented in the easy-to-follow context of the CLEAR structure, suggesting how to provide great coaching at the beginning, in the middle and at the end of coaching, and coaching style conversations.

Chapters 12–15 constitute Part 3, 'Coaching Conversations to Improve Clinical Care'. Chapter 12 looks further at the use of coaching approaches in clinical mental health work with service users and carers. I also highlight that there are circumstances where a direct coaching approach would not be appropriate. I indicate how coaching aligns very well with the concept of personal recovery.[5] In addition, this chapter considers coaching in the context of the two-way links between mental and physical health. Chapter 13 describes a case example that illustrates some of the points presented in Chapter 12.

Chapter 14 explores the role of coaching in co-production and co-creation of services, whereby people using mental health services partner with those responsible for designing and delivering them. I offer a case study about coaching in the co-production of a carer group (a group of people caring for those with mental health problems/learning disability). In Chapter 15, the subject of psychological trauma is discussed in relation to coaching.

The focus of the fourth and final part of the book is 'Coaching within Mental Health Care Organizations'. Chapter 16 explores coaching culture. In particular, I pay attention to internal coaching – that is, where an organization employs coaches to coach colleagues, rather than hiring in coaches who do not work within the organization. I present a case example of an internal initiative in a mental health organization, including some of the procedures and practicalities. Chapter 17 maintains a focus on internal coaching, looking in particular at ethical considerations. The discussion is brought to life by additional case studies.

The book concludes with a round-up of some key points, ideas about the future of coaching in mental health care settings, and consideration of what you will take away from your read.

My aim is for this book to be interesting and useful for people working in a range of roles (both clinical and non-clinical) in mental health settings. If you are one of those people, I hope it will help you build on what you are doing already and encourage you to have frequent and effective coaching style conversations in your everyday work. I mean conversations with your colleagues, with staff you manage and, when appropriate, with service users and carers according to your role. Also, I suggest that formal coaching sessions for mental health service staff can support their effectiveness, development and contentment. These coaching sessions can be delivered successfully by trained coaches employed within mental health care organizations.

I am glad you have decided to read this book – thank you! I am optimistic that you will put some of what you read into practice.[6]

Notes

1 To become a professional certified coach with the International Coaching Federation, it is necessary to successfully complete at least 125 hours of coach specific training with robust documentation (including a focus on ethics), provide 500 hours of formal coaching, undergo detailed evaluation of coaching performance and pass a written online exam. See https://coachfederation.org/credentials-and-standards/pcc-paths.

2 *Coaching psychology* refers to the 'enhancement of well-being and performance in personal life and work domains, underpinned by models of coaching grounded in learning or psychological theories and approaches' (adapted from Grant and Palmer, 2002, as cited in Green and Palmer, 2019).

Positive psychology has been described as 'The study of the conditions and processes that contribute to the flourishing (well-being) or optimal functioning of people, groups and institutions' (Gable and Haidt, 2005).

Occupational/organizational psychology is concerned with the performance of people at work and with how individuals, small groups and organizations behave and function. Its aim is to increase the effectiveness of the organization and improve job satisfaction of individuals. See https://careers.bps.org.uk/area/occupational (accessed 20 July 2021).

3 Conversations with Mike Slade, Professor of Mental Health Recovery and Social Inclusion, University of Nottingham, and Errol Green, Noushig Nahabedian and Patience McLean, Slam Partners, South London and Maudsley NHS Foundation Trust.

4 Email correspondence with Rob Briner, Professor of Organizational Psychology, Queen Mary University of London (July 2020). Conversation with Adrian Furnham, Adjunct Professor at BI Norwegian Business School and Professor at University College London (May 2020).

5 For further information on recovery-focused coaching training programmes for mental health practitioners, you may be interested in contacting slampartners@slam.nhs.uk.

6 In this book, I use 'they' as a singular personal pronoun throughout. 'They' has been in everyday use for centuries and is a lot more streamlined to read than 'he/she/person who doesn't identify as male or female'.

Mainly, I refer to the conversational partners in coaching style conversations and coaching sessions as coaches and coachees. I appreciate that coachee is a rather ugly word with a done-to quality, but it is clear in signifying the person who is the focus of a coaching conversation. Where coachees are people using mental health services, I tend to use the phrase service users.

The case studies and cameos presented in this book are fictional, drawing on broad and blended elements of experience.

References

Bird, V., Leamy, M., Le Boutillier, C. et al. (2014) *REFOCUS: Promoting Recovery in Mental Health Services*, 2nd edition. London: Rethink Mental Illness.

Briner, R.B. (2012) Does coaching work and does anyone really care?, *OP Matters*, 17: 4–11.

Dowling, T. (2006) I did it their way, *The Guardian*, 16 October. https://www.theguardian.com/lifeandstyle/2006/oct/16/healthandwellbeing.timdowling (accessed 24 June 2021).

Gable, S.L. and Haidt, J. (2005) What (and why) is positive psychology?, *Review of General Psychology*, 9 (2): 103–10. https://doi.org/10.1037/1089-2680.9.2.103.

Green, S. and Palmer, S. (eds.) (2019) *Positive Psychology Coaching in Practice*. Abingdon: Routledge.

Grover, S. and Furnham, A. (2016) Coaching as a developmental intervention in organizations: A systematic review of its effectiveness and the mechanisms underlying it, *PLoS ONE*, 11: e0159137. https://doi.org/10.1371/journal.pone.0159137.

Hawkins, P. and Smith, N. (2013) *Coaching, Mentoring and Organizational Consultancy: Supervision, Skills and Development*, 2nd edition. Maidenhead: Open University Press.

International Coaching Federation (ICF) (2020) *2020 ICF Global Coaching Study: Executive summary*. Lexington, KY: ICF. https://coachfederation.org/app/uploads/2020/09/FINAL_ICF_GCS2020_ExecutiveSummary.pdf (accessed 24 June 2021).

Passmore, J. (ed.) (2014) *Mastery in Coaching: A Complete Psychological Toolkit for Advanced Coaching*. London: Kogan Page.

2 Coaching fundamentals

Introduction

There is no one way to coach. But all the effective ways involve a set of key abilities. This chapter offers fundamentals for coaching and coaching-style conversations, both generally and in the field of mental health care. These coaching fundamentals are applicable to both the clinical and the non-clinical functioning of mental health care organizations.

This chapter is presented in four sections. The first explores eight principal coaching competencies. According to the International Coaching Federation, these are the skills and mindsets required by coaches to provide good coaching (ICF, 2019). A fictional case study (based on a blend of real coaching situations) is used to illustrate how a coach might put the coaching competencies into action. In this section, I also emphasize that there are times when a coaching approach will not be appropriate.

Having a good rapport with a coachee creates a context in which these competencies can flourish. The second section of the chapter draws on the work of psychologists Laurence and Emily Alison, as I look at how to promote strong rapport and productive communication.

Next, I remind readers that coaching is essentially about facilitating resourcefulness, and not about rescuing. I suggest that people who coach should get to know the Drama Triangle (Karpman, 1968) and Winner's Triangle (Choy, 1990) and keep them in mind. These models are useful in a broad sense to aid our understanding about some patterns of human interaction. The models can also help a coach to recognize if they tilt away from a facilitating role.

In the final section, I consider how ineffective coaching can be avoided. I stress that people providing coaching, but without mental health training, should not attempt to undertake the work of mental health practitioners.

Before I describe the competencies that coaches require, it is important to say that coaching and coaching style conversations are suitable only when the coachee feels sufficiently emotionally robust to engage in the process. After all, the work they will do with their coaches will invariably bring up some important challenges.

To benefit from coaching, people do not need to possess wonderful emotional and mental health. But at the time of a coaching conversation, to get the most from it, they *do* need to be able to think clearly enough to engage and see possible ways forward.

Mental health practitioners who use coaching approaches successfully in clinical contexts heed this fact. Of course, people seeking mental health care are very likely, at least initially, to be experiencing considerable mental suffering and many will be feeling intensely vulnerable. They may be emotionally wounded, desperate, addicted, fearful and/or unable to think as they usually do. I argue that, although not straightaway, many of these people can make good use of clinical care that involves a flexible coaching approach. At first, however, other clinical assistance will be more appropriate, such as practical support and a purely compassionate listening ear with tailored psychological and medical input.

At a later point, a coaching style that involves more goal-setting, planning and a greater degree of constructive challenge can be introduced to a service user's clinical care if they want that. By that time, hopefully, they will be able to think more clearly and feel increasingly reconnected with their own resourcefulness.

With this caveat in mind, let us move on to examine core coaching competencies.

Core coaching competencies

Good coaches demonstrate abilities, attitudes and ways of working that are captured in the International Coaching Federation's (ICF) list of eight core coaching competencies. During formal coaching sessions, coaches should use all these competencies purposefully. In day-to-day coaching style conversations, they also matter.

The updated ICF core competencies (effective 2021) are summarized below.

1. Demonstrates ethical practice in coaching. Ethical practice is about doing the right thing and responding wisely and well to complex situations that lack straightforward solutions. Issues of confidentiality, boundaries, safety and respect are often at the heart of a focus on ethics in coaching (as in mental health care). Those working in the field of mental health care receive training and develop detailed awareness about the importance of integrity, honesty and other aspects of professionally ethical behaviour. They are therefore likely to be well placed in relation to this coaching competency (see also Chapter 17 on the subject of ethics in coaching).

2. Embodies a coaching mindset. This refers to the development and maintenance of a mindset that is open and flexible and focused on the needs of the coachee. A coaching mindset involves acknowledgement that coachees are responsible for their own choices. Coaches should reflect on their own practice, be aware of what they are qualified to do and what they are not, and take steps to continue their own professional development. They should also seek help from others as necessary. They need to be mindful of context and culture in relation to themselves and other people, and consider the influence of their own emotional state on their coaching work.

3. Establishes and maintains agreements. Clear agreements about the nature and purpose of the coaching relationship are required, so that coach, coachee and any other people involved have a common understanding. Agreement should be reached about process, plans, goals and also practical and logistic issues such as the boundaries of confidentiality and planned duration of the arrangement. Many mental health practitioners and managers will be experienced in setting up and maintaining collaborative contracts.

4. Cultivates trust and safety. The ability to establish trusting professional relationships is crucial. To make progress, coachees need to feel comfortable to think and speak openly. A coach should demonstrate respect for a coachee's identity and make efforts to understand their perspectives, values and beliefs.

5. Maintains presence. In its definition of this competency, the ICF states that the coach should be 'fully conscious and present' with the coachee. Whilst that is a statement of the obvious, coaching will not work well unless the coach truly concentrates and genuinely engages with curiosity. The coachee needs to see and feel that the coach is doing this.

6. Listens actively. To listen actively involves more than hearing what is said. It means focusing on what the coachee is communicating with their words and in other ways. Brief reflection and accurate summary by the coach can help to clarify understanding for the coachee.

7. Evokes awareness. When coaches evoke awareness, they facilitate learning and insight by coachees. This can be achieved with the help of techniques such as powerful questioning, remaining quiet, using metaphor and appropriate challenge. Particular coaching tools may be relevant. The coach should be prepared to adjust and tailor the approach to help coachees get the most from conversations. When awareness is evoked, people can stretch further to make progress and explore new viewpoints.

8. Facilitates client growth. This last competency concerns how coach and coachee should work together to use the coachee's learning and new awareness to set measurable goals and plan actions. Any progress should be acknowledged to reinforce successes.

The case study below brings core coaching competencies more to life. (There will be further discussion of coaching competencies 'in action' throughout the coming chapters.)

Case study: Jo's story

Jo was widowed suddenly at the age of 38. She was an experienced mental health nurse whose role had always been in direct clinical care as part of a large health service. After taking leave for several months, Jo met with her senior manager, Mia, to consider next steps in relation to work. During her time off, Jo had decided that she did not want to return to clinical work. In fact, by then 39 years old, Jo was seriously contemplating the possibility of leaving not only the organization, but nursing and the field of mental health care completely.

Jo's senior manager, Mia, suggested Jo speak to a qualified coach employed within the organization. Jo accepted this offer and met with the coach for three sessions. It was not the coach's job or agenda to persuade Jo in any particular direction. He ensured that this fact was understood by Jo and Mia.

The coach empathically supported Jo to think about her work situation. These work-related coaching conversations followed a structure (the nature of which we will discuss in later chapters). But they needed to take place at Jo's pace, along a path she chose and with specific consideration of her needs and circumstances. The plan was that the coaching sessions could provide Jo with a 'safe', timely space in which to think about her present and future, with the coach as a steady companion.

Jo noticed that she felt 'more able to think constructively instead of going round in circles' because of her coach's pattern of inquiry. He asked simple (but not easy) questions, then stayed attentively quiet as she pondered her answers. For example, she found that the question 'What is the most pressing issue for you to resolve now?' helped her to focus and reflect systematically. Jo liked it that her coach seemed to understand that Jo was, as she put it, 'sort of okay but sort of not okay at the same time'.

At an early stage in the coaching, Jo talked about her decision not to go back to clinical work and she stated this would probably mean choosing a new career outside the organization. Over the course of several conversations together, the coach helped Jo to examine what she wanted professionally, asking questions such as: 'Where does work fit for you at this point?' and 'What matters most to you about your work?' He supported Jo to deliberate bravely, to consider possible options and to notice her assumptions. 'Leaving nursing is one option, what might be some others to explore?'

For Jo, an important aspect of the coaching work entailed coming to her own clear conclusion that she did, in fact, want to continue to be involved with nursing, although not in direct clinical care. Jo firmed-up this conclusion after the coach prompted her to further explore her core values, needs, attributes and strengths. Jo explained that a meaningful, future professional role for her would 'ideally involve somehow supporting nurses and nursing leaders to do their jobs really well, whilst still maintaining their well-being'. The coach offered an observation that this sounded 'almost like a mission statement' – Jo agreed that was right. Very significantly for Jo, she had the sense that her husband who had died would 'completely back me with this mission statement'. For Jo, the coaching process seemed to bolster her self-confidence and motivation: it helped to remind her of her strength and energy.

Jo had some further meetings with her senior manager, Mia, who cared about Jo and also was mindful of Jo's extensive nursing skills and experience. The organization was facing major difficulties in recruiting and retaining nursing staff and was undergoing some restructuring.

When meeting with Mia, Jo discussed her ideas and hopes about her professional life that had emerged during coaching. It became clear that there was opportunity to trial a way forward that might suit Jo and address organizational needs. Mia proposed that Jo apply to contribute to some projects which were not directly clinical – that is, providing input to a new mentoring and development programme for nurses and aspiring nurse leaders.

Jo went on to take up this part-time role in the promotion of nursing professional development. She upheld her personal 'mission statement', which fitted well with organizational goals. Moving forward a year: Jo was finding her work fulfilling, it was valued and Jo was acquiring new skills. In relation to broader aspects of Jo's life, she continued to feel the pain of her bereavement. But over time the nature of her pain changed, and became (for the most part) easier to live with. Jo was pleased she had remained in nursing and believed that the coaching had supported her to make decisions, goals and plans.

Box 2.1: Coaching competencies demonstrated by Jo's coach

Demonstrated ethical practice in coaching. The coach was sensitive to Jo's situation and grief, and the importance of confidentiality. He was aware of the organizational context but was focused on supporting Jo to explore what she, herself, wanted. (See Chapter 17 for more on ethical considerations.)

Embodied a coaching mindset. The coach was clear that Jo was responsible for her own conclusions and decisions. He was careful to keep within his coaching remit, yet mindful of Jo's wider circumstances.

Established and maintained agreements. The coach ensured shared clarity between coach, Jo and the manager about the scope, practicalities and boundaries of the coaching.

Cultivated trust and safety. The coach was genuine and respectful, making efforts to understand Jo's standpoint whilst acknowledging that he could not know exactly how Jo was feeling.

Maintained presence. The coach was consistently attentive and 'fully there' with Jo, and this promoted her confidence in the coaching process and in the coach.

Listened actively. The coach was closely attuned to Jo's communication throughout. He was sparing and selective in what he himself said, and he harnessed the power of silence so that Jo had 'room' to think.

Evoked awareness. The coach asked effective, carefully chosen questions. He undertook a specific line of inquiry with Jo to help her clarify some ambivalent ideas about her future professional direction, and to explore her values, attributes and strengths.

Facilitated growth. The coach worked with Jo to help her shape these ideas and explorations into plans, taking account of her realizations about her strengths and values.

Connection in coaching conversations

If a coach is to successfully employ the core competencies discussed above, it is vital that rapport is established. In this section, I draw on the work of forensic psychologists Laurence and Emily Alison, as described in their book *Rapport:*

The Four Ways to Read People (2020). The authors explain that if we are to promote effective human connection, we should prioritize what they call HEAR in our communication. HEAR stands for: honesty, empathy, autonomy and reflective listening.

Box 2.2: The HEAR acronym: The Alisons' cornerstones of rapport

Honesty involves being direct yet not too blunt. This requires bravery and discernment.

Empathy[1] is about understanding somebody's point of view and considering/sensing what emotions may be underlying it. It is worth noting that being empathic does not always necessitate being emotionally warm towards, or being in agreement with, the other person. (Although in coaching, it almost always helps the process if the coach is affable.)

A sense of **Autonomy** and free choice for the coachee is part and parcel of coaching. By and large, humans do not like being told what to do or being forcefully pressured to respond in a certain way.

Reflective listening is, of course, an important skill for coaches. It comes more naturally to some than others, and the crunch ability involves reflecting back key points concisely for the coachee to elaborate on.

Creating rapport between a coach and a coachee hinges on the coach cultivating a natural sense of different communication styles – that is, their own and that of the person in front of them.

Alison and Alison put forward a model to aid understanding of communication styles. They outline four types, each one represented by an animal:

- cooperation (monkey)
- confrontation (T-Rex)
- capitulation (mouse)
- control (lion)

Each of these styles has a 'good' (constructive, adaptive) aspect and a 'bad' (unhelpful, maladaptive) aspect (see Box 2.3). It is relevant to think about this model in the coaching context, as we all tend to habitually use some styles more than others. It can be interesting to consider which animal archetypes ring the loudest bells, so to speak, in terms of our own most frequent good and bad communication styles (for me, it is 'good monkey, bad mouse'). We can also think about which animal archetype we need to gain more competence with (my 'good lion' is coming on nicely these days).

> **Box 2.3: The Alisons' animal archetypes to aid understanding of communication styles (paraphrased)**
>
> *Good monkey* – cooperative and warm
> *Bad monkey* – overemphasis on being friendly
> *Good T-Rex* – frank, clear and no messing about
> *Bad T-Rex* – attacking and threatening
> *Good mouse* – shows humility and tolerance
> *Bad mouse* – vacillating and unassertive
> *Good lion* – confident and decisive
> *Bad lion* – dominant and overbearing

In other words, it is useful for coaches to be aware of which 'animals' are in the room at any given point. To be sure, to achieve the best communication across a range of situations in life, at one time or another we will need to use all of these styles – and sometimes a blend of them – in a versatile way.

But the main point here for coaches is awareness. When a coach accurately recognizes and takes into account a coachee's predominant communication style, the coaching will be more effective.

Coaching in mental health settings: facilitation not fixing

Attention to core competencies and rapport will take a coach a long way towards successful coaching. I also want to specifically emphasize that people who coach most effectively do so in a way that helps to ultimately empower the coachee and promote their agency.

Many mental health practitioners have a head start in becoming great coaches, as they already possess qualities needed for good coaching, such as an interest in the meaning and motivation of people's behaviour. But mental health practitioners may also have a tendency to want to rescue the person they are coaching, rather than to help boost that person's own problem-solving skills. A tendency to fix – rather than to facilitate – can put a huge spanner in the works of effective coaching.

Practitioners using coaching as part of their clinical approach should therefore remain aware of six principles of coaching for mental health. These are adapted from work by Jenny Rogers and Arti Maini (Rogers, 2012; Rogers and Maini, 2016).

1 Service users are resourceful
2 The practitioner's role is as enabler rather than expert
3 The service user's mental health will be affected by what is going on in their life as a whole, so the practitioner should take a whole-life approach

4 The service user sets the agenda for the conversation

5 Practitioner and service user are equals in the conversation

6 Coaching is about change and action

In this context of 'facilitation not fixing', it is useful to explore two triangle models drawn originally from the psychoanalytic field of transactional analysis (TA). Transactional analysis focuses on understanding people's interactions and behaviour in terms of roles they adopt, not necessarily consciously, when interacting with others.

I show below, that in coaching and in life, we are well advised to move away from a Drama Triangle model and towards what is called the Winner's Triangle.

The Drama Triangle

The Drama Triangle (Figure 2.1), developed originally in the 1960s by Stephen Karpman, highlights three roles: rescuer, victim and persecutor.

1 *Rescuer* – the shining hero role, the one who saves

2 *Victim* – the powerless one who's on the receiving end of whatever happens, but who may also have a manipulative tendency

3 *Persecutor* – the bully role, the blamer and the punisher

At the core of the model is the idea that we all adopt roles in a partly unconscious attempt to get our needs met. The drama that follows as roles are played out is often unhelpful and hinders constructive interaction, progress or problem-solving.

Let's consider the following, far from ideal, clinical relationship as it unfolds over time. The practitioner, call him Robert, adopts a rescuer role (needing to be needed and not taking account of the pressure involved in being a 'shining hero'). This in turn contributes to the service user, call her Becca, assuming a greater victim role (vesting power and rescuing capacity in Robert, and not making her own decisions).

Figure 2.1 A version of the Drama Triangle

Rescuer and victim have 'top billing' in this drama. The more Robert plays the part of the rescuer, the more Becca plays the part of victim. As time goes on, Robert is not being nearly as helpful as he likes to think, and he is starting to feel stressed by all the effort required to maintain his hero role.

You may know the old saying (variations of which apparently crop up in many cultures): 'Feed a man a fish and you feed him for a day – teach him to fish and he feeds himself for life'. In our context here, it is as though Robert keeps feeding Becca fish without helping her to find ways to catch them herself, and without even checking whether she wants fish … or, even, might prefer something else.

Then the drama shifts: Becca feels let down by Robert. Metaphorically, he is not providing her with the quantity or quality of fish she expected, and she becomes angry with him. Becca shifts roles from victim to persecutor (in reality, threatening to report him to managers as incompetent). Robert feels hurt and stunned, and subsequently adopts the victim stance himself.

Then more drama: Robert does not feel at all at home in the victim role and without thinking it through, he turns to adopt a persecutor role. He unconsciously tries to regain control and take a one-up position in a vain attempt to feel better. He becomes a hectoring 'expert' in his interaction with Becca: this is not good. For example, Robert chides, 'Well, you have not taken your medication have you – why is that?'

Has all that drama been of use to Becca? Perhaps early on when she felt particularly vulnerable, some rescuing by Robert seemed helpful. Pretty soon, however, the limits of that helpfulness were reached with negative effects for both Becca and Robert. They played out their roles with little conscious awareness of how the roles were unfolding and getting in the way of progress.

Suggestion for you

Think of a time during an interaction with someone else where you took on one of the drama triangle roles. Be completely straight with yourself about this. Given what you know about the Drama Triangle, what could you have done differently?

The Winner's Triangle

The Winner's Triangle was developed by Acey Choy and represents a more constructive pattern of roles and interactions than those of the Drama Triangle, as you will see in Figure 2.2. Coaching competencies come to the fore in the Winner's Triangle model. If we notice that we are heading towards involvement in a Drama Triangle dynamic, it is useful to consider how we can help shift the situation towards a Winner's Triangle dynamic instead, as demonstrated in Box 2.4.[2]

Figure 2.2 A version of the Winner's Triangle

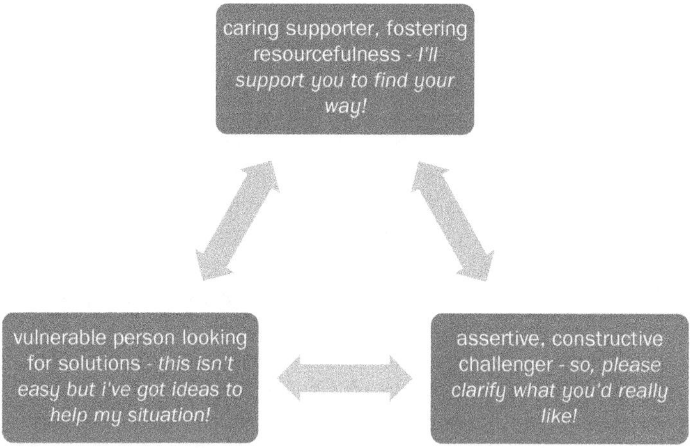

caring supporter, fostering resourcefulness - *I'll support you to find your way!*

vulnerable person looking for solutions - *this isn't easy but I've got ideas to help my situation!*

assertive, constructive challenger - *so, please clarify what you'd really like!*

Box 2.4: Drama Triangle to Winner's Triangle

Drama Triangle	becomes	Winner's Triangle
Rescuer	becomes	**A person offering caring, authentic support, enabling others to develop their own resourcefulness.** The former rescuer is in touch with their own needs and does not say 'yes' to every request or demand – this is valuable for their own self-care and for the person they are saying 'no' to.
Persecutor	becomes	**A constructive challenger who is assertive but not bullying or blaming.** The former persecutor directs energy towards clarifying and solving problems, not being punitive.
Victim	becomes	**Someone finding their own way forward, whilst in touch with their vulnerability.** The former victim accepts their own vulnerability for what it is and they can move on to discover some personal resilience and strength. There is greater ability to use their own resourcefulness, and less risk of manipulation.

Coaching: when the wheels come off

Some basic propositions can help avoid having 'the wheels come off' during a coaching session, thus keeping our coaching work on the right track. Whatever our professional training, we need to know the limits of our knowledge and skillset. Coaches without a mental health background should avoid straying outside their coaching remit and into clinical mental health care territory.

Everyone in any kind of coaching role will, inevitably, at times encounter coachees who are sad, worried, angry or otherwise emotionally distressed. If that emotional distress is extreme or persistent, then attempting to actively coach that person at that time would be ill-judged (as mentioned earlier), even if the coach has mental health training and experience.

How should coaches respond to a coachee presenting with a significant mental health issue (given, of course, that each situation is individual)? As you would expect, the typical advice is for the coach to be calm, collaborative, honest and respectful. They should remain mindful of potential safety issues and be aware of relevant systems, services and available options if additional support is needed.

Returning to consider more routine coaching conversations, much of what an effective coach does involves stimulating the coachee's thinking and ongoing reflection. The coach supports the coachee to think about what is within their control and influence, while remembering that it is possible to be both realistic and aspirational at the same time. Coaches should resist becoming drawn into discussing details about other people not present, and they should be alert that this can be surprisingly tempting. When skilful questions are asked in a timely way that resonates for the coachee, then the coaching journey is likely to continue on a good track.

Boxes 2.5 and 2.6 highlight what coaches should and should not do to ensure 'the wheels don't come off'.

Box 2.5: What the coach should do

The coach should:

- ✔ Contract well
- ✔ Respect the contract/agreement about the purpose of the conversation
- ✔ Pay attention to trust or rapport
- ✔ Be consistently present for the coachee
- ✔ Focus on process rather than details of content
- ✔ Really listen and talk sparingly
- ✔ Focus on what is within the coachee's control or influence
- ✔ Mainly be in the present moment or look to the future
- ✔ Support the coachee in seeking possible solutions
- ✔ Use *what, how, who* and *when* questions more than *why* questions
- ✔ Remember what they are there for (it's not to win a 'nicest coach of the year award')

✔ Remember what they are there for (it's not to win a 'cleverest coach of the year award')
✔ Notice rather than interpret
✔ Hear the solutions that the coachee comes up with for their problems
✔ Facilitate the coachee to find and articulate their own ways forward
✔ End the conversation well

Box 2.6: What the coach should be careful to avoid

The coach should avoid:

✗ Contracting in a sloppy way
✗ Overlooking the contract/agreement about the purpose of the conversation
✗ Overlooking the importance of trust and rapport
✗ Being preoccupied with their own *stuff* and not being present for the coachee
✗ Getting drawn into the juicy content of the conversation rather than being with the coachee in the coaching process
✗ Talking too much and failing to really listen
✗ Talking in depth about people who are not there
✗ Becoming caught up in the coachee's past, rather than being mainly present and future focused
✗ The conversation becoming more about problems than possible solutions
✗ Asking too many *why* questions – *what, how, who* and *when* questions are often preferable
✗ Being too eager to be liked
✗ Being too eager to seem clever
✗ Interpreting rather than noticing
✗ Thinking they know the solutions
✗ Explaining what they think are the solutions
✗ Ending the conversation in a sloppy way

Competent coaches know that the coaching process is all about the coachee and the alliance, not all about the coach. Indulgent ego massage should not be part of the picture for either coachee or coach during these discussions. And lastly, in our efforts to provide great coaching, we should remember to end coaching conversations well, finishing both strongly and clearly.

Having covered some fundamentals for powerful coaching, in Chapter 3 we continue to explore how coaching fits, and what it can add, in relation to other interventions and forms of conversation.

Notes

1 The concept of empathy is complex. Psychologists Paul Ekman and Daniel Goleman have discussed three types: cognitive empathy, emotional empathy and empathic concern. *Cognitive empathy* refers to the ability to see things from another's perspective, whilst *emotional empathy* implies seeing things from the other's perspective and connecting with some of the associated feeling. *Empathic concern* relates to compassion, and the wish to ease the perceived suffering of the other. (See Daniel Goleman, 2015 on the different kinds of empathy.)

   In relation to our ability to perceive the emotions of others accurately, it is worth noting the comments of neuroscientist Lisa Feldman Barrett (2018): '... emotions that you seem to detect in other people actually come in part from what's inside your own head. And this is true in the courtroom, but it's also true in the classroom, in the bedroom, and in the boardroom'.

2 In relation to the Drama Triangle and constructive alternative ways of interacting, see Emerald (2016).

References

Alison, E. and Alison, L. (2020) *Rapport: The Four Ways to Read People*. London: Vermilion.

Barrett, L.F. (2018) You aren't at the mercy of your emotions – your brain creates them, *TED Talk*, 13 January. https://lisafeldmanbarrett.com/2018/01/13/ted-talk-you-arent-at-the-mercy-of-your-emotions-your-brain-creates-them/ (accessed 25 September 2021).

Choy, A. (1990) The Winner's Triangle, *Transactional Analysis Journal*, 20 (1): 40–46. https://doi.org/10.1177/036215379002000105.

Emerald, D. (2016) *The Power of TED* (*The Empowerment Dynamic)*, 10th anniversary edition. Edinburgh: Polaris.

Goleman, D. (2015) Daniel Goleman on the different kinds of empathy [video], *YouTube*, 22 October. https://www.youtube.com/watch?v=WdDVvLEKoc8 (accessed 25 September 2021).

International Coaching Federation (ICF) (2019) *ICF Core Competencies*. Lexington, KY: ICF.

Karpman, S.B. (1968) Fairy tales and script drama analysis, *Transactional Analysis Bulletin*, 7 (26): 39–43. https://karpmandramatriangle.com/pdf/DramaTriangle.pdf.

Rogers, J. (2012) *Coaching Skills: A Handbook*, 3rd edition. Maidenhead: Open University Press.

Rogers, J. and Maini, A. (2016) *Coaching for Health: Why It Works and How To Do It*. Maidenhead: Open University Press.

3 Coaching and related interventions

Introduction

In this chapter, I explore what makes coaching distinct from, and similar to, other forms of intervention. In coaching, as in all interventions, we should seek to understand the cultural perspectives of others, and try to be self-aware about our own worldview and biases.

First, I consider psychological therapy. It is a given that when someone accesses psychological therapy they are usually not feeling mentally robust and sometimes their thoughts are jumbled. To make the most of a coaching conversation, however, the person requires a 'good enough' level of mental robustness and sufficient capacity for clear thinking. That said, the methods of coaching and therapy can often overlap.

Next, I look at other interventions such as mentoring, supervision, consultation and teaching. I argue that dividing lines cannot always be rigidly drawn between coaching and its cousins. Some, such as mentoring, are more closely related to coaching than others, for example consultation.

I then outline some concepts that are supported by evidence and that inform coaching and related interventions. I believe that when coaches work in step with these concepts, their coaching will have greater positive impact and their practice will have greater credibility.

The chapter concludes with an exploration of the importance of cultural considerations in relation to coaching.

Cousins: coaching and psychological therapies

Definitions of coaching and psychological therapy tell us that the former has a focus on inspiring people to maximize their personal and professional potential. The latter helps them to bring about change and enhance their well-being in the face of mental and emotional problems, challenges or illness.

I have heard it claimed, wrongly in my opinion, that therapy involves delving into the significance of the past, whereas coaching looks only to the future. This is a false dichotomy. Whether engaged in therapy or coaching, it is often necessary for a person to see and acknowledge where they have been so they can make informed choices about where they want to go next and how they might get there. The emphasis on a forward-looking focus does tend to be stronger in coaching than it is with many forms of therapy.

Psychological therapy and coaching do share common ground. Psychological therapy is about more than assisting with the management of emotional and mental symptoms or helping to release people from them. Successful psychological therapy involves a journey towards a meaningful and functioning life as defined by the person living it, and in this respect, it is like coaching. It is feasible for someone to access separate coaching sessions during a period in which they also receive therapy and/or take psychotropic medication.

From my perspective, coaching has much of its basis in types of psychological therapy and counselling. Cognitive behavioural therapy, solution-focused therapy, person-centred counselling, and acceptance and commitment therapy, amongst other modes, have all given a great deal to the world of coaching. This is evident when we consider these therapeutic approaches: cognitive behavioural therapy (CBT) involves exploring, challenging and shifting our thinking, feelings and behaviours to help manage our problems. Solution-focused therapy emphasizes creating solutions by building on a person's strengths, resources and hopes for the future. Person-centred counselling highlights that practitioners should demonstrate genuineness, care, acceptance and empathy towards the people with whom they are working. Acceptance and commitment therapy (ACT) promotes the importance of values and prompts people to accept their thoughts and emotions, instead of trying to struggle with them. I believe that qualified mental health practitioners can combine therapy and a coaching style effectively when that is appropriate, in a flexible and blended style of working.

Both coaches and therapists need supervision (see below) to enable them, amongst other things, to see what they are personally bringing to the process and to reduce the risk of becoming 'tangled up' in ways that are not useful for the person engaged in coaching or therapy.

I ought not leave the subject of psychological therapy without reference to trauma. The effects of trauma present in a variety of guises and are a frequent focus for therapy. Difficulties associated with trauma can likewise emerge during coaching but they will not necessarily be obvious. Trauma-related distress can wax and wane, can have unforeseen triggers, can cause unanticipated suffering and can interrupt coaching progress. Trauma and the coaching context will be discussed in Chapter 14.

Other interventions related to coaching

Let me lay out the key features of mentoring, supervision, consultation and teaching one by one, to show how they compare to coaching. These interventions are related to coaching, but with some differences.

Mentoring

We can think of coaching as a journey where the coach says, 'Where do you want to go, how could we get there, how will you know you've arrived?'

In contrast, we can think of mentoring as a journey where the mentor says, 'Where do you want to go, how could we get there? I've got suggestions about the route and can tell you about the landscapes ... I've been there before'.

A mentor is often a senior colleague or person in the same or a similar organization. The mentor draws on the benefit of their own knowledge and experience to offer guidance for the mentee, and can make suggestions they may not have thought about on their own. This can support the mentee to develop and progress. My experience is that in practice, coaching and mentoring are not always strictly delineated, but coaches do need to be vigilant and notice if they slip into mentoring. Depending on the circumstances, an element of mentoring may or may not be appropriate. Some merging is more likely when the coach has expertise in the subject that the coachee brings for discussion. Box 3.1 shows some differences and similarities between coaching and mentoring.

Box 3.1: Differences and similarities between coaching and mentoring

Coaching	Mentoring
Usually no explicit guidance (coach does not necessarily require knowledge/experience in the area talked about)	More guidance (mentor has knowledge/experience in the area talked about)
Usually a shorter-term arrangement	Usually a longer-term arrangement
Both coaching and mentoring have a role in promoting professional development	
Both coaching and mentoring promote constructive reflection	

Consultation

Consultation is a term that refers to the provision of advice and expertise. In the business world, for example, consultants are frequently hired to help organizations improve their business performance, increase profit, and improve management and strategy. Consultants act as experts, whereas coaches do not usually.

The title of consultant is a notable professional one, particularly in the field of medicine. It is used by doctors who are knowledgeable and experienced with recognized credentials for their senior medical role. Consultant psychologists, nurses and other consultant practitioners are at similarly senior levels in their professions.

I have an expert hat (a metaphorical one) to wear some of the time in my role as a consultant psychiatrist. However, that hat is often to be found on its figurative peg when I am having a coaching style conversation with service users, carers or colleagues.

In summary, a way in which pure consulting differs from pure coaching is that consulting routinely requires substantive expertise in the particular subject area under discussion.

Supervision

Supervision often refers to a special type of attentive mentoring offered to those undertaking work with people that is difficult or complex. Supervision can allow professional standards and quality to be reviewed and maintained. It promotes learning, can inspire practitioners, and can support their strength and capacity to continue with work that may feel daunting.

Supervision offers a space for reflection, in which practice can be comprehensively examined from different angles and developed with attention to effectiveness and safety. 'Helicopter view' is a term that is used to describe the perspective supervision provides.

Coaching and supervision are not the same. Supervision usually involves providing oversight and guidance whereas coaching does not customarily entail giving advice. In summary, we can think of supervision as having three main purposes: to offer support, to foster development and to review the quality of the work.

Teaching

Alain De Botton describes teaching as a fundamentally important process for humans involving the transfer of significant 'ideas from one mind to another' (The School of Life, 2018). This description highlights the difference between teaching and coaching. Coaching is not about getting an important idea from one mind into another. It is about creating a context so the coachee's mind generates its own important ideas and learning. The teacher passes their knowledge to the person being taught, the coach helps to unlock or kindle the knowledge within the person being coached.

Of course, teaching is a crucial skill, vital in multiple situations, not just in education settings. In Alain De Botton's words, good teachers display the following characteristics: 'they do not blame someone for not already knowing, they can admit that they do not know lots of things, and they pick their moments'. Generally speaking, the same applies to good coaches.

Concepts that inform coaching and related interventions

In recent years, research has proliferated about the systematic application of psychological and learning theory to improve life experience, work performance and well-being. This is the field of coaching psychology. The use of such concepts, and models that are supported by evidence, can assist coaches to be more effective thinking partners, helping coachees to harvest the benefits of a rich coaching experience.

The following list highlights, in brief, six examples of concepts that inform coaching practice.

Cognitive theory. This theory, developed by Aaron Beck in the 1970s, proposes that the way we feel and how we behave is influenced by our perception of events and situations (Beck, 1976). It is not so much the actual events and situations, it is the meaning and interpretation we give to them that affects us. Cognitive behavioural approaches have been extensively studied in recent decades and are supported by research. I believe cognitive theory is foundational to coaching.

Self-determination theory. Psychologists Edward Deci and Richard Ryan have emphasized that as humans we have an inner drive to reach our full potential (Ryan and Deci, 2000). This self-motivation and our mental well-being are enhanced when we make our own choices (autonomy), connect with other people (relatedness) and have a sense of being effective (competence). The human spirit can be diminished or crushed if our feelings of autonomy, relatedness and competence are stifled; it is strengthened if they are promoted. Coaching can promote them.

PERMA model. One of the founders of positive psychology, Martin Seligman, developed this model. Positive psychology emphasizes the promotion of psychological wellness rather than emphasizing the curing of psychological illness. The PERMA model involves attention to five interrelated core elements in the consideration of psychological well-being and happiness (Seligman, 2012):

P = Positive emotion (notice contentment and joy, cultivate positive, grateful attitudes)

E = Engagement and flow (discover and do things you love doing)

R = Relationships (connect with others)

M = Meaning and purpose (do what matters to you and has personal meaning)

A = Achievement (strive for what is important, appreciate your accomplishments)

Strengths theories. In short, work undertaken by Martin Seligman and Christopher Peterson produced strengths theories which declare that we feel better and function more effectively if we play to our personal strengths (Peterson and Seligman, 2004). The term 'strengths' encompasses positive personality traits, talents, skills, interests as well as external supportive resources (Green and Palmer, 2019). The exploration and further cultivation of personal strengths is a key component of coaching. We can usefully work *with* our personal strengths, work *on* our potential strengths and work *around* resistant areas of limitation that we may have (Furnham, 2020).

Transtheoretical model of behavioural change. James Prochaska and Carlo DiClemente identified that we go through a series of stages of change as we shift to adopt different behaviours (Prochaska et al., 1994). The stages are:

- Pre-contemplation
- Contemplation
- Preparation
- Action
- Maintenance

The stages are not as clear cut as a list implies, but it is a useful model and links with motivational interviewing[1] (see Chapter 12). Motivational interviewing is a way of communicating that helps people explore and address situations they may be brushing under the carpet or feel ambivalent about, such as unhelpful habits or addictive behaviours. It is useful for coaches to have the transtheoretical model in mind if they are having coaching style conversations with people facing, ignoring or part-wanting change.

Three Circles Model of emotional regulation. Psychologist Paul Gilbert proposed that we have evolved three systems of emotion regulation which relate to each other (Gilbert, 2009). These are:

- A system to give us feelings of drive, excitement and vitality (drive mode)
- A system to give us feelings of contentment, safety and connection (soothing mode)
- A system to give us feelings of anger, anxiety and disgust (threat mode)

The systems can become out of kilter. We become stressed and distressed if we spend too long in drive and threat modes, and we can rebalance by shifting more to soothing mode, cultivating self-compassion. Coaching provides people with an opportunity to consider this issue of balance and the steps they can take to regain it if necessary and to maintain it.

Coaching, cultural competence, cultural humility

In broad terms, the word culture means 'the values, beliefs, thinking patterns and behavior that are learned and shared and that [are] characteristic of a group of people'.[2]

Our cultural identities help to shape our ongoing behaviour. For example, we can consider the impact of heritage, gender, religion or age on communication styles and family roles. The ways in which people perceive health and illness, how we cope with adversities, and how we seek support and treatment are influenced to a considerable degree by cultural factors.

Cultural competence can be 'loosely defined as the ability to understand, appreciate and interact with people from cultures or belief systems different from one's own' (DeAngelis, 2015). The concept of cultural competence is applicable to individuals, groups, teams and organizations, and it involves an ongoing developmental process. Shifts towards cultural competence require thoughtful communication skills.

The International Coaching Federation advocates core values of, 'Integrity, excellence, collaboration and respect', and states, 'We will recommit ourselves to valuing the unique talents, insights and experiences that every coach and client brings to the world' (ICF, 2020).

We can espouse and sign up to important aspirations. And crucially, day to day at a personal level, we need also to continuously notice, reflect and adapt so we can acquire greater cultural competence.

It is not easy to face the too-often grim narratives of how we humans have treated one another, and we can resolve to seek to understand others' perspectives. When we do not look to understand each other's point of view, we are more likely to miscommunicate and misconnect. This understanding needs to be more than an intellectual one. Understanding another's perspectives is not necessarily the same as agreeing with them.

In the coach role and more broadly, we need to figure out our own cultural position and identity in addition to educating ourselves about the cultural identities, insights and standpoints of the people we are with.

The cultural backgrounds of both the coachee and the coach influence the coaching process: both people bring a cultural identity to the conversation. It is a mistake, of course, to assume that if a coach and coachee have one or two cultural factors in common (like both being women from London) that they will be on the same wavelength about many things.

It is worthwhile for us to undertake an honest, no-holds-barred personal exploration of the stereotypes and biases we all harbour, both positive and negative. Sometimes we do not realize we have a habit of pigeon-holing people in a certain way. The stereotypical views we hold can influence how we work as coaches and in our other roles – sometimes in subtle, but nonetheless significant, ways. I am aware that being a white British woman in my fifties shapes my blind spots and biases, and I need to continue in my efforts to learn about and be aware of these.

Suggestion for you

Observe in yourself any stereotypical views (positive or negative) you might hold about the following, and consider how they might possibly sway you (even slightly) in your role as coach:

- A man in his twenties with a tattoo on his forehead
- A middle-aged male headteacher
- A female politician of a right-wing party

The progress of a person or an organization towards cultural competence can be gauged with reference to James Mason's Continuum of Cultural Competence (Mason, 1995). This describes five progressive stages with 'cultural destructiveness' at the negative end and 'cultural competence' at the positive end. An individual or organization in a position of cultural destructiveness demonstrates attitudes and practices detrimental to people and their cultures. Individuals and agencies at the positive end of the continuum accept and respect cultural differences, are self-reflective and seek to learn. Wherever we are currently on this continuum in our roles in mental health settings, and as coaches, let's proceed on our life-long journeys along the road towards cultural competence with our eyes open.

So, the concept of cultural competence serves as a reminder to us to strive to learn about and understand other communities. The idea and term of cultural humility (the ability to maintain a stance of openness to others) is preferred by some, given that it is not fully possible to become thoroughly competent in the culture of other people. Both concepts are valuable (Greene-Moton and Minkler, 2020).

Black, Asian and Minority Ethnic (BAME) is a term used in the UK at the time of writing to describe anyone from a non-white background, and includes people from a range of ethnic, religious and cultural circumstances. In relation to accessing mental health care or coaching approaches, people from BAME backgrounds may encounter cultural and language barriers as well as barriers such as institutional racism in the health care system and structural racism within wider society.

In addition to seeking better understanding of our own and others' backgrounds, it is also important for us to reflect on the effects of power dynamics, historical inequalities between different cultures and disparities in levels of privilege.

Coaches and/or mental health practitioners may lack understanding of experiences that are significant for someone from a BAME background. Practitioners may not be able to realize truly what it is like to suffer discrimination or minoritization,[3] and (as previously discussed) they can consciously or unconsciously exercise bias. Some people may be reluctant to seek mental health care or coaching due to a sense of stigma or shame, which may be more marked in some BAME communities (Rethink Mental Illness, 2020).

Seeing a practitioner or coach from a similar background may be helpful for some. I believe it is necessary to increase the diversity amongst coaches and mental health practitioners, especially as our society is becoming increasingly diverse. I re-emphasize that practitioners should be open to ongoing learning about relevant aspects of someone's culture to help shape the coaching process collaboratively and appropriately. The ICF core coaching competencies are, by definition, crucial for effective coaching (see Chapter 2).

In Chapter 4, we will begin to focus more attention on the subject of coaching models and techniques.

Notes

1 Motivational Interviewing Network of Trainers (MINT). https://motivationalinterviewing.org (accessed 10 July 2021).

2 Cultural identity theory. https://www.communicationtheory.org/cultural-identity-theory/ (accessed 21 July 2021).
3 Minoritized individuals and populations are those 'whose collective cultural, economic, political and social power has been eroded through the targeting of identity in active processes that sustain structures of hegemony' (Selvarajah et al., 2020, cited in Dutta et al., 2021: 192).

I am grateful to Dr Arti Maini of Imperial College London, School of Public Health, for her helpful input to the final section of this chapter. Dr Maini is co-author (with Jenny Rogers) of *Coaching for Health: Why It Works and How to Do It* (2016).

References

Beck, A.T. (1976) *Cognitive Therapy and the Emotional Disorders*. New York: Penguin.

DeAngelis, T. (2015) In search of cultural competence, *Monitor on Psychology*, 46 (3). https://www.apa.org/monitor/2015/03/cultural-competence (accessed 21 July 2021).

Dutta, N., Maini, A., Afolabi, F. et al. (2021) Promoting cultural diversity and inclusion in undergraduate primary care education, *Education for Primary Care*, 32 (4): 192–97. https://doi.org/10.1080/14739879.2021.1900749.

Furnham, A. (2020) *Psychology 101: The 101 Ideas, Concepts and Theories that Have Shaped Our World*. London: Bloomsbury.

Gilbert, P. (2009) *The Compassionate Mind: A New Approach to Life's Challenges*. London: Constable.

Green, S. and Palmer, S. (eds.) (2019) *Positive Psychology Coaching in Practice*. Abingdon: Routledge.

Greene-Moton, E. and Minkler, M. (2020) Cultural competence or cultural humility? Moving beyond the debate, *Health Promotion Practice*, 21 (1): 142–45. https://doi.org/10.1177/1524839919884912 (accessed 25 September 2021).

International Coaching Federation (ICF) (2020) *ICF publishes Statement of Diversity, Inclusion, Belonging and Justice*. Lexington, KY: ICF. https://coachingfederation.org/blog/icf-publishes-statement-of-diversity-inclusion-belonging-and-justice (accessed 21 July 2021).

Mason, J.L. (1995) *Cultural Competence Self-Assessment Questionnaire: A Manual for Users*. Portland, OR: Portland State University, Research and Training Center on Family Support and Children's Mental Health. https://www.pathwaysrtc.pdx.edu/pdf/CCSAQ.pdf.

Peterson, C. and Seligman, M.E.P. (2004) *Character Strengths and Virtues: A Handbook and Classification*. Oxford: Oxford University Press.

Prochaska, J.O., Norcross, J.C. and DiClemente, C.C. (1994) *Changing for Good: A Revolutionary Six-Stage Program for Overcoming Bad Habits and Moving Your Life Positively Forward*. New York: William Morrow.

Rethink Mental Illness (2020) *Black, Asian and Minority Ethnic (BAME) mental health*, last updated August 2021. https://www.rethink.org/advice-and-information/living-with-mental-illness/wellbeing-physical-health/black-asian-and-minority-ethnic-mental-health/ (accessed 25 September 2021).

Rogers, J. and Maini, A. (2016) *Coaching for Health: Why It Works and How To Do It*. Maidenhead: Open University Press.

Ryan, R.M. and Deci, E.L. (2000) Self-determination theory and the facilitation of intrinsic motivation, social development, and well-being, *American Psychologist*, 55 (1): 68–78. https://doi.org/10.1037/0003-066X.55.1.68.

Seligman, M.E.P. (2012) *Flourish: A Visionary New Understanding of Happiness and Well-Being*. New York: Free Press.

Selvarajah, S., Deivanayagam, T.A., Lasco, G. et al. (2020) Categorisation and minoritisation, *BMJ Global Health*, 5: e004508. https://doi.org/10.1136/bmjgh-2020-004508.

The School of Life (2018) How to be a good teacher [video], *YouTube*, 1 March. https://www.youtube.com/watch?v=-FkvBA3U5lg (accessed 21 July 2021).

4

The use of coaching models and techniques

Introduction

Coaching models are conversational frameworks that support the coaching process. These methods and frameworks can make it more likely that a coachee will get from where they are at the start of coaching to where they would like to go. There are a variety of techniques and so-called tools that can be incorporated into coaching practice, making it more powerful.

In this chapter, I point out that whilst coaches should make good use of models and techniques, these have their limitations. Coaching frameworks and tools need to be employed thoughtfully in line with context. Coaching achieves more when it involves a personalized process rather than a formulaic one – when it fits for a coachee like bespoke tailoring rather than something off the peg.

In the first section of the chapter, I argue that coaching models should not be centre-stage in a conversation. The coachee should specifically occupy that spot, setting the agenda with what is important for them. Self-awareness on the part of the coach is vital if they are to use coaching models well.

I then offer some reflections and also caveats about the use of coaching models and techniques. The conversation should have flow and space, but the coach needs also to provide some conversational structure and boundaries to help to keep the experience on course. An example of this is the requirement for the coach to have a close eye on time in relation to progress along the coaching journey.

Emotions can be seen as important messengers during the coaching process. Regardless of the coaching model or techniques used, the coach must respond in an agile fashion to the emotional landscape of a conversation. In relation to this, I expand on the subject of mindfulness and coaching.

The chapter concludes with a word of caution about slavish goal-directedness. While goals are often key in coaching, too much focus on the desired destination can obscure the importance and value of the journey. Moreover, if each individual step along the way does not receive sufficient attention, the goal is less likely to be attained. And sometimes, the vagaries of life mean a goal becomes less relevant as we work to achieve it, and we may need to change course.

Coaching models with a light touch

There is a profusion of coaching models, frameworks and tools that can be employed to scaffold and enhance coaching conversations. The different models often share much in common. Models are an important aspect of good coaching, but coaching involves more than the implementation of models. Coaching that stimulates a coachee to think effectively is quite a skill, not just a process of following a set of moves or questions. There is no magic-spell formula for a great coaching conversation.

Excessive insistence by the coach on following a complicated coaching framework can lead to a conversation where the connection between coach and coachee becomes superficial and important threads may go unnoticed or undeveloped. It can be as though the coach is not truly there. Instead, they are in their own head mentally skimming down a list of prompts for what they 'should' ask next while attempting to sieve the conversation through the model or vice versa. If the coach starts to congratulate him or herself inwardly about employing the model very well, or starts to feel inadequate because the conversation has detoured from the model, then they risk not listening to the coachee.

When a coaching model is applied in a natural and flexible way, it does not intrude. This increases the chances that the coaching conversation will take on a flow of its own and sometimes glide along. For the coach, when this happens it feels like there is hardly any heavy lifting to be done, and the coachee is likely to gain from the conversation.

A great coaching conversation can be like a great painting. A painting can take us on a mental journey, yielding unexpected thoughts, powerful emotions or old memories. When we study a painting, it prompts us to look at details close-up and then stand back to see the big picture. We pause and reflect, decide what we like and what we find less appealing about the details of the artwork. Sometimes, we imagine (regardless of whether we are artists or not) what we would do differently or what we would love to paint instead. We can feel uplifted.

An unobtrusive, well-designed picture frame and mount can help to bring out the best in a painting. Yet we may not even notice the frame and mount at all when we look at the picture. That is how it can be with a strong coaching conversation. The conversational content is like the painting and the coaching model is like the frame.

Regardless of the model that a coach is using, self-awareness is critical. A coach must not let eagerness to use a model get in the way of their self-awareness. It is an interesting irony that when we have greater awareness about how we are 'being', the more we can get done. In other words, self-awareness is linked with more effective 'doing'. Self-awareness is very different to self-absorption. When we are self-aware, we usually have a better understanding of the world outside ourselves. We become more other-aware and more world-aware too. (There is a discussion of mindfulness later in the chapter.)

Coaches should show up as human beings as well as human doings during the coaching process. If not, the trusting alliance that is at the heart of the interaction will not develop properly, and there is a risk that coach and coachee will be out of tune with one another. In the absence of authentic rapport, a coach's use of even the most elegant coaching models may fall flat and prove uninspiring.

Conversational structure and boundary

Coaching models can be seen as containers in which coaching conversations take place. A model helps to provide structure and boundaries for a conversation.

The amount of structure in each coaching session needs to fit with what is most useful for the coachee. Coachees often feel comfortable with a balance in relation to the extent to which the conversation is shaped and the degree to which it is 'free-ranging'. They want neither too little nor too much structure for the interaction. Too little can jeopardize a productive future focus. For example, this is likely to occur if the coachee becomes fixed on recounting and venting repeatedly about a frustrating past scenario. On the other hand, too much structure can get in the way of expansive thinking and exploration, such as when the coach adheres to a set of favourite coaching questions and jostles the coachee down the list. The optimal level of structure varies from person to person and for the same person from one conversation to the next.

A Chinese proverb, often referred to by coach Claire Pedrick, points out: 'The Banks of the Yangtze give it depth, drive and direction' (Pedrick, 2020). Similarly, the boundaries and structure of a coaching conversation give it depth, drive and direction. For example, throughout a coaching conversation, the coach should be consistent about the length of time available, and should help to maintain the coachee's journey through the stages of a chosen model.

It is useful to see a boundary as the start of something rather than a restriction. As George Eliot wrote in *Middlemarch* ([1871/72] 1993), 'Every limit is a beginning as well as an ending'.

Coaching models, emotions and mindfulness

A coach's best intentions to use a coaching model may be scuppered and rendered irrelevant by a coachee's strong emotions. In such a case, the coach should be conversationally nimble and empathic. The intended use of a particular coaching model may need to be paused or dropped if a coachee requires time and space to 'release' their upset and express their distress. We all know that powerful feelings can seize us. They can catch coachees out and leave them temporarily unable to think, hear or apply reason. Emotions sometimes have the capacity to derail coachees during a coaching conversation at alarming speed. On the other hand, emotions sometimes fire motivation, creative energy or inspiration.

In recent years, the work of psychologist and neuroscientist Lisa Feldman Barrett and others has indicated that we have more control over our emotions than at first it might seem. Barrett explains that our emotions do not 'happen' to us, rather we construct our emotions based on our experiences and sensations. Her work refutes ideas that we may be at the mercy of specific emotional circuits in our brains. The lesson is that over time and with practice, we can change our emotional life by training our brains to construct different emotions – what Barrett (2018) calls being the 'architect of your experience'. This is a hopeful message. I would recommend that you read Barrett's work to get your head around the concepts. I found some of them challenging initially, as they seem to run counter to some traditionally held ideas about human emotions.

A coachee's feelings need to be factored into the judicious use of any coaching model. During coaching conversations, emotions can be valuable emissaries conveying clues as to what is important to a coachee and what needs to happen next. These are crucial messages to heed in a coaching discussion even if it means deviating from a chosen model. When there is a surge of emotion for the coachee, the coach may ask in their head, and sometimes even out loud, 'Where did that come from?'

It is relevant here to consider the concepts of mindfulness and compassion in coaching. Mindfulness is about being intentionally and fully present in the moment. It is impossible to properly understand mindfulness without practising it to some extent. When we train in mindfulness, we become more aware of what is going on with our thoughts, feelings and physical sensations. This helps us work with them rather than being overwhelmed by them. The hope is that we gain greater insight into our emotions, develop ability to focus better, and in turn experience the benefits that may follow from this, for example, improved relationships.

Compassion involves being sensitive to our own suffering and that of others, along with a strong sense of wanting to lessen and prevent that suffering. I will specifically mention self-compassion. This is not self-pity or self-indulgence and it is not letting ourselves off the hook. When we develop more compassion for ourselves, we can be genuinely more open-hearted towards other people too. Self-compassion allows us to be more honest with and accepting of ourselves. Being compassionate can involve giving feedback or messages that are difficult for ourselves or others to hear. It is not about being soft or namby-pamby.

Knowledge and understanding about the fields of mindfulness and compassion practice cannot be achieved by studying the concepts alone. Experiential learning is key alongside any conceptual learning. Sitting meditation is not the only way to strengthen mindfulness skills; being focused and mindful moment by moment as we, for example, clean our teeth, walk up the stairs or go about other day-to-day activities, all contribute. In terms of the benefits of mindful habits, there are rarely any rapid shifts but over time we start to 'get it', realize we are relating to the world a bit differently, and notice that some positive changes are underway by degrees.

Let me invite you to experience, and be reminded about, an aspect of mindfulness: paying open, curious attention.

Suggestion for you

- **Look** for a few moments at your hand. Really look at it. The skin, the nails, the bony bits, the shapes and bending of your fingers.
- **Move** your hand slowly, bring your fingers to touch and move on your thumb.
- What are you **sensing** on the surface of and within your hand? On the outside in contact with the air? On the inside amongst the bones and warm blood?
- Now, if it does not seem too weird or schmaltzy for you, think of some of the times your hand has **done something kind** for someone, or for an animal. Summon up a sense of kind caring energy in your hand. You may want to close your eyes for a moment while you do this.
- Then place your hand on a part of your body that could do with some *warm, kind energy*, rest it there and take a few deep breaths.

Coach and author Liz Hall speaks of how a mindful compassionate approach to coaching involves cultivation (by both coach and coachee) of awareness, body wisdom and compassion. Body wisdom refers to being in tune with our body and 'listening' to what it tells us. To keep these elements in mind we can think of ABC (Hall, 2015).

We are all individual in terms of how we react and respond to the world and to others in it. Some people almost always want to think things through in detail, and others rely more on feelings and gut reactions. Of course, it would be inaccurate to label people as either thinkers or feelers, but those who deliberate a lot may not find the concept of getting in tune with body wisdom that helpful or meaningful. At least, not at first.

Nonetheless, I think it is worthwhile for all of us to spend some time and effort in the development of our capacity to be aware of what is going on within ourselves and around us, in the present moment.

The evidence for the use of mindfulness-based approaches to enhance well-being and functioning continues to expand. There is an emphasis on the use of these approaches in clinical mental health care as well as a mushrooming of non-clinical mindfulness programmes. For example, an adaptation of mindfulness-based cognitive therapy (MBCT) for depression (Segal et al., 2018) to a programme that is designed for people not suffering with mental disorder, MBCT for Life (Strauss et al., 2021).

Mindfulness and compassion-based understanding provide us with opportunities to perceive situations, others and ourselves more clearly. This helps us set goals that are aligned with our values and strengths. And goals aligned with our values and strengths are always going to be a better fit for us. So, although coaching that focuses on mindfulness may not be predominantly goal-oriented, relevant goals do indeed emerge. We have a greater chance of success when we pursue aims that resonate with what we are most 'in touch' with. And if we do not achieve those aims, then mindfulness and compassion can support us to respond in ways that:

(a) do not make things worse (which let's face it is what we often tend to do when we are thwarted) and

(b) allow us to move on in a constructive direction.

Coaches should have an understanding about psychological trauma, and be aware that some mindfulness exercises may be unsuitable, or require adaptation, for coachees experiencing the effects of trauma (see Chapter 14).

Before leaving, for now, the areas of mindfulness and compassion, it is notable that their associated benefits can be achieved without making the process about spirituality. Mindfulness can be embraced in secular contexts potentially acceptable for people of all faiths and none, with appropriate respect for all spiritual and religious perspectives. Having said this, secular mindfulness is not without its critics.

Goals and coaching models – a word of caution

Many coaching models have an understandable focus on the importance of goals. Striving towards worthwhile goals is important. Yet, achieving a precise future goal is not usually the be all and end all of coaching or of life. Having eyes only for that goal can mean missing the richness of the path towards it, and may result in failure to consider properly what might unfold after it has been achieved. There is a danger in the mistaken view, 'When I achieve *that*, *then* I'll be happy', whatever *that* is.

Naturally, end goals are often hugely important; yet the direction of travel can be even more significant or meaningful than the final destination. Our big ambitious goals are usually attained through numerous small steps and choices. Constantly imagining the hoped-for end-point without carefully attending to all the necessary tiny paces along the track to it may mean we never actually get there.

Some self-help and coaching books express an almost tyrannical level of positivity about our ability to achieve awe-inspiring outcomes. There are coaches advocating particular coaching models who claim, unrealistically, that their favoured techniques almost always lead to sure-fire success for coachees. Some coaches strongly discourage the use of phrases like, 'I'll do my best to reach this goal'. They claim that 'I'll try' should be struck from the vocabulary and replaced with 'I will succeed' or forceful can-do statements which put full emphasis on the end-point outcome. Their message is that you can achieve your dreams if you want them enough and if you try hard enough: well, the truth is that sometimes you can't. We should view such enthusiasm through a 'real world' lens. As psychologist Susan David (2017) says, 'When we push aside normal emotions to embrace false positivity, we lose our capacity to develop skills to deal with the world as it is, not as we wish it to be'.

Of course, there are goals which we feel must be met, and I appreciate the value of an optimistic attitude for sure. We should remember though, if we think we can insist on certainty and success, then we are not living in the real world. Yes, we want to achieve our goals – and it is a fact of life for all of us that sometimes we do not attain them as we had planned. It is worth remembering that we can still move forward even if we do not get what we want, or if we do not want what we get.

Coaches can facilitate a coachee's awareness about a good choice of goal and how best to achieve it.[1] Struggling to attain an ill-chosen goal can have an ongoing, negative impact on well-being. People need to consider carefully if they really want to pursue a goal that they hope will bring them eventual happiness, if during the pursuit of that goal they feel consistently miserable.

Coaching can also promote a coachee's awareness that life may dish up something totally unanticipated: but, nonetheless, things can be okay, or even a great deal more than okay. A coach's use of coaching models needs to take into account that life is rife with uncertainty.

Having taken an overview of some of the advantages and issues to be aware of in relation to coaching frameworks and techniques, in the next chapter I discuss some coaching models.

Note

1 On the subject of goals, I will comment briefly about the well-known SMART goal acronym. Many people can reel off 'Specific, Measurable, Achievable, Relevant, Timebound', yet when it comes to writing a SMART goal they may well come up with a woolly aim instead of a crisp, deliverable, punctual and pertinent objective. When we set a SMART goal, for this to be a truly valuable exercise, we need to ensure that we have addressed each of the five components. Naturally, not all of our goals in life fit with a SMART approach. But the ability to define SMART goals properly is a valuable one to acquire and implement.

References

Barrett, L.F. (2018) *How Emotions are Made: The Secret Life of the Brain*. London: Pan Macmillan.

David, S. (2017) The gift and power of emotional courage, *TED Talk*, November. https://www.ted.com/talks/susan_david_the_gift_and_power_of_emotional_courage (accessed 21 July 2021).

Eliot, G. ([1871/72] 1993) *Middlemarch*. Ware: Wordsworth Classics.

Hall, L. (2015) *Coaching in Times of Crisis and Transformation: How to Help Individuals and Organizations Flourish*. London: Kogan Page.

Pedrick, C. (2020) *Simplifying Coaching: How to Have More Transformational Conversations by Doing Less*. London: Open University Press.

Segal, Z.V., Williams, M. and Teasdale, J. (2018) *Mindfulness-Based Cognitive Therapy for Depression*, 2nd edition. New York: Guilford Press.

Strauss, C., Gu, J., Montero-Marin, J. et al. (2021) Reducing stress and promoting well-being in healthcare workers using mindfulness-based cognitive therapy for life, International *Journal of Clinical and Health Psychology*, 21: 100227. https://doi.org/10.1016/j.ijchp.2021.100227.

5 Three coaching models

Introduction

Having covered some general points about the use of coaching models in Chapter 4, here I outline and explore three valuable coaching models and approaches. The models inevitably share similar aspects though they also have some of their own distinctive features.

I begin by briefly discussing the popular goal-based GROW model developed by John Whitmore (1992). This model has a focus on goals and provides scope for reflection, enabling the emergence of insights and planning.

I then talk about two coaching models which I have found particularly useful in my own coaching practice. One is the CLEAR framework (Hawkins and Smith, 2013), which offers a means to consistently shape coaching conversations in a flexible and forward moving way. This model anchors the second part of the book, and you will become very familiar with it – if you are not already so. The other is the ThinkOn® approach (Gilbert and Chakravorty, 2015). Like the GROW model, ThinkOn includes a focus on goals, and is well suited to coaching situations where clear goals and planning are to the fore. ThinkOn supports coachees to relate to problems in a solution-focused way.

In my work, I have used the CLEAR model and elements of the ThinkOn approach in combination during many effective coaching conversations in mental health contexts. I will show how ThinkOn principles can fit well within the broad structure afforded by the CLEAR framework.

The GROW model

GROW is a well-known model established by Sir John Whitmore several decades ago. The letters in the word GROW stand for the steps of a coaching conversation or series of conversations. It is a structure that can be used in a range of coaching style interactions, and used one-to-one or with a number of people together. The steps are as follows, and the coachee is invited to explore each area of inquiry.

G = Goal – what do you want?
R = the current Reality – where are you now?
O = the Options for moving from the current reality towards the goal – what could you do?
W = the Way forward – what will you do/when/with whom?

GROW is readily grasped and remembered. The straightforward name of the model conveys its lack of multiple or complicated stages, and this is one of its strengths. It is particularly useful when coaching involves an emphasis on performance goals and results.

Let's now walk more slowly through the four letters in GROW. It is fundamental to get the **G** – the goal – right. When the coachee is vague about their goal or is struggling to accurately articulate it, it may be necessary to spend considerable time clarifying this. This process of clarifying what the coachee really wants may by itself be the main task of the coaching conversation.

Coach and coachee need to ask if achieving a named goal will really result in what is wanted and required? As Stephen R. Covey (1989) pointed out, climbing a ladder that is leaning against the wrong wall gets us to the wrong place. Choosing the right goal is about giving proper thought to where we lean our ladder. Also, it may be that we need to reposition our ladder over time.

I had some conversations when I started as a coach that turned out to be more 'Grrr' than GROW because I was pushing the coachee too hard and too fast to define their goal.

The **R** part of a coaching conversation based around the GROW model also needs careful attention. Exploration of the **R** – that is, the current reality – can risk the coachee getting stuck with their familiar 'script' of an often repeated story which keeps them looking backwards to the past. An overemphasis on past detail can hinder future focus. Future focus (whilst acknowledging previous life lessons) is key to coaching. As we were told when we were children … 'Look where you are going!'

O stands for 'options' and certainly not for 'ought to' – that is, the coach does not say 'I think you ought' to do such and such. Instead, the coach facilitates the coachee to generate their own possibilities. The coach resists the urge to add their two pennies' worth, and keeps the way clear for the coachee to cultivate their self-belief and creativity.

W, denoting the way forward, keeps the focus on the intended outcome and future planning. The coachee focuses on **W** when they have progressed through the first three stages to arrive at this point. Coaches neglect **W** at their peril. This last part of the GROW model is often seen in basic terms of tasks to be done and actions to be implemented. The **W** may, however, be less concrete than a plan of clear action steps. It may involve capturing a realization which points to a new route ahead, but which is, as yet, not fully clear.

The CLEAR model

The CLEAR model was developed by Peter Hawkins and Nick Smith. The five letters represent guidance that propels and shapes a coaching conversation.

C = Contract (agree the intention, the ground rules and open the conversation well)

L = Listen

E = Explore
A = Action
R = Review (close the conversation well with an agreed plan)

The CLEAR model can be thought of as a three-stage process, although it contains five elements:

Contract ⇒ **L**isten and **E**xplore ⇒ **A**ction and **R**eview

C = Stage 1. This involves getting off to a strong start: a coaching session can stand or fall on this, and the tone of the whole interaction can be set from the very start. In coaching, the term 'contracting' refers to establishing a shared agreement between coach and coachee (and sometimes others, like a manager) about the focus and hoped for outcome of the coaching.

Contracting includes agreeing what the coaching activity will involve and how it will take place. A focus on establishing the coaching contract is pivotal early on in the engagement. Contract agreements are often reviewed and adjusted as the coaching progresses in line with what is emerging for the coachee. It is not unusual for a coachee to come to a coaching conversation with a degree of vagueness about what they want to get from it, so fathoming the contract carefully, and subsequently re-contracting as necessary, may take time: and it is time well spent.

When coach and coachee meet for a series of conversations or sessions, it is often useful to recap and catch up briefly at the start of each conversation about action plans agreed at the last one and the progress made. However, that does not mean rehashing all that was previously discussed.

L, E = Stage 2. This is the middle, open stage where the person expresses, explores, expounds, expands and experiments. The coach listens a lot and asks relatively little, in line with having two ears and one mouth. During this part of the conversation, it is vital for the coach to keep out of the coachee's way as they think. The coach is likely to come up with many potential questions, but only the best, most relevant of these should be put to the coachee.

When coachees have a strong sense of trust in the coaching relationship and there is empathic rapport, they are empowered to be true to themselves and make deeper discoveries. In this part of CLEAR, the coachee may survey a broad view and clarify just where they fit within it, and then they may choose to examine finer grain details from a variety of perspectives.

AR = Stage 3. This is the stage where aspects of the conversation are drawn together and it is brought to a close. The expansion and sense of possibility present during Stage 2 is gathered in to allow a focus on summarizing what has emerged and the intention that follows on from this. In many conversations, specific action points and tasks will be formulated during this latter part of the interaction.

In other coaching discussions, the emphasis in Stage 3 is more on collating reflections and deciding not to make definite action plans at the time. A conscious decision not to decide right now about exactly what to do is a plan in its own right. The contracting stage provides the first bookend, as it were, for the conversation and the second bookend is supplied at the end of the action/review stage. Both bookends are needed to adequately support what goes in between. Closing a coaching conversation well is as vital as opening it well.

Clear Sky (the CLEAR model as air travel)

Let's consider the three stages described above using an analogy of air travel. Claire Pedrick developed and elaborated on an air travel analogy in her book, *Simplifying Coaching* (2020).

- take-off (stage 1, Contracting)
- the flying through the sky part (stage 2, Listening, Exploring)
- the landing (stage 3, Action, Review)

From my perspective, here is a potted version of CLEAR in terms of a plane journey.

Before the point of take-off, it is important that both the coachee and the coach are aware of the intended destination – that is, the intended outcome for the conversation today … 'We're flying together today to Brussels'. (Alternatively, the conversation might represent more of a talk with the travel agent to explore where a suitable destination would be.)

During the flight, there is scope for relaxing into the journey, seeing things from new vantage points, and opening the mind – that is, exploring possibilities and options as in … 'You may unfasten your seatbelts … to your left you can see a spectacular view of the Alps'. (Clearly, there is no geographical accuracy in the analogy here.)

Quite a while before the plane comes in to land, the coachee needs to know they should prepare for the end of the trip – that is, that the session is drawing to a close and it is necessary to consider what will come next … 'We'll be starting our descent shortly, fasten your seat belt for landing. Please ensure that all luggage is stored in the overhead locker etc.'.

The coaching focus and process needs to feel right for the person coming for coaching if it is to be successful. It is not useful for the coach to think along the lines of, 'It's always a good idea to go via Heathrow – I've been that way before and it was great. Yes, we'll do that'.

Both coachee and coach may be surprised about where the coaching conversation goes. Initially, they are bound for Oslo and they unexpectedly detour to Leeds Bradford. This sort of thing happens sometimes. And, strangely, Leeds Bradford may turn out to be just the right place for that person on that day.

A coachee might want to focus on career goals in a coaching session but find to their surprise, they end up talking a great deal about their mother. This may actually be very relevant, but was not what they had anticipated at the outset. Having said that, coach and coachee both need to ensure the track of the conversation remains related to the agreed goal (even if not in a straightforward way).

I'll conclude this focus on CLEAR by saying that, for me, it is a model that feels very natural. It offers a framework for reflective and potentially transformative conversations or meetings. Techniques and elements of other models can be readily incorporated within the overall CLEAR format. In Part 2 of the book, I will present coaching guidance in a detailed way using the CLEAR structure as a scaffold.

The ThinkOn® approach

Andy Gilbert, who founded ThinkOn®,[2] describes coaching as 'a process that facilitates change and development; helping individuals and teams invent the future ... increasing performance and making a difference'.

This solution-focused approach to coaching is based on the pragmatic ThinkOn Key Thinking Principles, as developed in the 1990s by Andy Gilbert and Ian Chakravorty (2015). Their aim was to improve the effectiveness of people's thinking, and in turn optimize the benefit of coaching. The seven key thinking principles are shown in Box 5.1 (with permission of ThinkOn®).

Box 5.1: The ThinkOn® Seven Key Thinking Principles

1 Have a **strong reason why** you want to make a difference
2 **Define your goal** before starting to make a difference
3 **Consider possibilities** and **plan your priorities** before taking action
4 Have **self-belief** that you can and will make a difference
5 **Involve others** to help you make a difference
6 **Take personal responsibility** for your actions
7 **Take action** and measure the results of the difference you make

---

The developers of ThinkOn chose these key principles after conducting hundreds of conversations with people who were in the process of achieving all kinds of goals, from running a long-distance race to implementing change in a large organization. The question that Gilbert and Chakravorty asked themselves as they undertook all those conversations was, 'What are the principles that people naturally use when they are successful at making a difference?'

The ThinkOn approach is pragmatic and helps people reflect, problem-solve and reach decisions. Systematic common sense is a powerful and elegant thing (and not necessarily all that common): most people benefit from a greater awareness of the ThinkOn principles listed above. Coaching conversations provide ideal opportunities for people to apply these principles well.

I am mindful of the ThinkOn principles along with the broad CLEAR structure when I am coaching. For example:

In the **C** (*contracting*) stage of a CLEAR conversation, it can be valuable for the coachee if the coach helps them to focus on the following ThinkOn principles:

- Have a strong **reason why** you want to make a difference – that is, check you really want to.
- Define your **goal** before starting to make a difference – that is, be clear about what you are trying to achieve.
- Check **self-belief** that you can and will make a difference – that is, make sure you think your goal is realistically achievable.

In the **L, E** (*listening and exploring*) stage of a CLEAR conversation, it can be valuable for the coachee if the coach helps them to focus on the following ThinkOn principles:

- Think of **possibilities and clarify your priorities** before taking action to make a difference – that is, explore a range of possible ideas and options.
- Think how to **involve others** to help you make a difference – that is, consider who might possibly help you and how they might benefit too.

In the **AR** (*action and review*) stage of a CLEAR conversation, it can be valuable for the coachee if the coach helps them to focus on the following ThinkOn principles:

- Take **personal responsibility** for your actions – that is, consider if you truly commit to follow through on actions you plan.
- Take **action** and measure the results of the difference you make – that is, decide what you will actually do and when. Decide how you will know if your actions have been successful.

Having explored a number of coaching models that can provide a shape and structure for conversations, in the next part of the book I will go into greater detail about how to make coaching really effective.

Notes

1 I am grateful for many useful conversations with Claire Pedrick.
2 ThinkOn® is also known as Go M.A.D.®, with Go M.A.D.® standing for Go Make A Difference. You may be interested in visiting https://gomadthinking.com/ and exploring the 'Thinking for Good' app.
    I'm grateful for helpful conversations with Andy Gilbert and Kath Roberts of ThinkOn.

References

Covey, S.R. (1989) *The 7 Habits of Highly Effective People*. New York: Simon & Schuster.

Gilbert, A. and Chakravorty, I. (2015) *Solution Focused Coaching*. Woodhouse Eaves: ThinkOn Books.

Hawkins, P. and Smith, N. (2013) *Coaching, Mentoring and Organizational Consultancy: Supervision, Skills and Development*, 2nd edition. Maidenhead: Open University Press.

Pedrick, C. (2020) *Simplifying Coaching: How to Have More Transformational Conversations by Doing Less*. London: Open University Press.

Whitmore, J. (1992) *Coaching for Performance*. London: Nicholas Brealey.

Part 2

Coaching Conversations with a CLEAR Scaffold

Introduction to Part 2

In Part 2, I offer tried-and-tested coaching techniques, questions and attitudes. These yield effective results in a range of coaching and coaching style conversations across a variety of contexts within the mental health and well-being field and more widely. Obviously, not all these ideas and tips will apply to all types of coaching style interactions, and discernment is needed about how and when to use different elements of this guidance.

Over the next few chapters, I discuss coaching skills in line with the overall order of CLEAR coaching conversations. I present coaching guidance according to the CLEAR framework (Hawkins and Smith, 2013), as this provides a logical way to offer the information.

Chapter 6 sets out coaching skills and knowledge that are especially useful for the **C** (*contracting*) stage, Chapter 7 for the **L** (*listening*) stage, Chapters 8 and 9 for the **E** (*exploring*) stage, and Chapters 10 and 11 for the **AR** (*action and review*) stage. However, I want to stress that the coaching points and ideas described in these chapters are certainly not exclusive to a particular part of a coaching conversation. For example, Chapter 7 focuses on listening skills that are relevant, of course, at each stage throughout the coaching process.

Reference

Hawkins, P. and Smith, N. (2013) *Coaching, Mentoring and Organizational Consultancy: Supervision, Skills and Development*, 2nd edition. Maidenhead: Open University Press.

6 | C is for Contracting: skills and knowledge

Introduction

Chapter 6 will look at the **C** in CLEAR. We know that it is valuable for coaching conversations to get off to a sound, authentic and upbeat start. This chapter offers some key learning points for effective contracting: it explores some aspects of the **C** phase of the CLEAR model, presented in four sections. I am not here focusing on all the formal and logistical aspects of agreeing a coaching contract, such as the basics of explaining confidentiality or discussing payment (if applicable). The assumption is that those aspects have been covered properly.

First, I demonstrate the value of beginning a coaching conversation with an end in mind. This involves clarifying where the coachee would like to be by the end of the conversation given the time available. They are likely to use the conversation well if they know what difference they would like it to make. The outcome they want may change as the conversation progresses and as different insights emerge. Therefore, re-contracting and revising the initially agreed goal is not at all unusual during a coaching conversation.

I then go on to suggest that it is useful for a coach to explore what form of discussion would most suit the coachee on that particular day. It is sensible for the coach to ask the coachee if they have a view about how the coach could best support them during the meeting. For example, would the coachee prefer the coach to push back and challenge a lot, or a little, or somewhere in between?

Readiness for the conversation, on the part of the coachee and also as demonstrated by the coach, is the focus of the third section of the chapter. Here, the coach asks the coachee to check in as to how they feel about the upcoming conversation, and to give consideration about where particularly they want to start it.

Finally, I look at the concept of 'starting where you are'. This section is rich in metaphor. When a coachee truly starts where they are, it means they meet their current reality and can honestly look it in the eye. I employ an ancient allegory to emphasize that wanting everything to be just right in order to feel okay is unrealistic. However, there is often much within our control, and it is normally wise to focus on these more tractable aspects.

And by the end of this conversation ...?

In a coaching conversation, both the coachee and coach benefit if they have clarity about the desired outcome. Working towards explicit goals often seems less tiring and confusing than the pursuit of fuzzy ones. When considering what outcome to aim for, we also do well to remember to choose the best goal ... not necessarily the first one that comes to mind.

If the coachee is not clear about the outcome they would like, then the conversation might focus on how they could best develop an understanding of what they do actually want, drawing especially on their strengths and values.[1] As mentioned in Chapter 5, the goal of a coaching discussion may be to define what the appropriate ongoing or big-picture objectives are.

The coach should inquire about goals routinely at the start of the session as a crucial part of the contracting phase. This helps focus the discussion and serves as a reminder about the need to use the time well. After a coachee has identified the outcome they want for the conversation, it is helpful for them to consider how they will know if they have achieved it or not. What will be the measure of their success by the end of the conversation or session? For example, they may decide they want to have a written action plan for completing a project, a list of key points to convey at an imminent meeting, or just a subjective sense of greater clarity about an issue they have been struggling to understand.

Time is an important factor here. If someone coming for a coaching conversation is tempted to off-load a lengthy, repetitive groan about their circumstances, the question, 'What would you like to be the outcome by the time we finish today at (such and such) time?' can help them prioritize and resist excessive distraction. There can be a place for a coachee's moaning in coaching, but if this complaining and negativity is unbounded, it can rapidly become the Japanese knot weed of constructive conversation. Having said that, sometimes a coachee may become very upset and there may be a need for them to vent their frustration or let a bout of tears take its exhaustive course. In these circumstances, the active coaching can be put on hold while the coach remains supportively alongside the coachee.

The coach needs to be sensitive about how the time set aside for the conversation is framed. Perception about the time available for coaching could be unconditionally optimistic, as in 'We have got a whole sixty minutes if we want it'. Conversely, the time-poor perspective would be: 'We have only got sixty minutes for this'. The perspective does make a difference.

We get more done when we embrace the attitude of, 'It's not too late if we start now'. Even with a few minutes of a coaching conversation remaining, there can be enough time for something valuable to crystallize out for the coachee. In fact, occasionally it can be amazingly productive when the thinking momentum surges in the closing section of a coaching session, the final furlong.

Discussions about goals are easily pulled off-course by coachees waxing lyrical about what they do *not* want, rather than getting down to the business of choosing what they really do want. For instance, a coachee may spend time lamenting, 'I don't want to keep falling out with the team about this issue'. The coach can explore flipping this statement into a question like, 'If you weren't falling out with the team about this issue, how would you be interacting with them about it instead?'

Goals, like the one expressed above, which start with the phrase 'I don't want to' are sometimes known as 'Dead Person's Goals' in acceptance and commitment therapy (Harris, 2009). The reason for this description is that the goal as stated could be achieved more reliably by a corpse than by a living person.

Suggestion for you

At the start of a one-to-one conversation that takes place over the next few days, experiment with some informal contracting. Check first with the other person that you have their agreement to try this. Ask them what they would like as an outcome by the end of the talk, and keep that in mind as the conversation goes on. (Obviously, choose a conversation where some experimental contracting will not just sound weird and out of place.)

A favourite coaching question: 'What would you like to be different by the end of this conversation?'

And how shall we 'do' this conversation?

'So today, am I wearing hobnail boots or fluffy slippers?' Intriguingly, a great coach asked me this within a few minutes of starting to coach me in a virtual conversation. This was not an invitation to make a guess about her footwear.

As coaching gets underway, it is worthwhile for the coach to gain an idea about what style of interaction might be most useful for the coachee. The obvious way to do this is to ask them. When coaching, I check up-front at the start if it is okay for me to interrupt occasionally during the conversation, and I clarify whether the coachee feels comfortable to be challenged. I invite them to tell me if/when they want to press the pause button on the session at any point. I also check out what they think about the prospect of an occasional suggestion from me. Sometimes a coachee seems keen for ideas from a coach, and at such times the coach should be particularly self-aware and measured. The expression by the coach of an occasional, tentative, 'take it or leave it' type of opinion is very different to showering a coachee with a flood of suggestions. The latter could slew the coaching conversation and block the coachee's thinking.

A favourite coaching question: 'How can I be most useful to you in this conversation?'

Readiness ...

A coaching conversation has a greater chance of going well when both coachee and coach feel ready for the conversation. By ready for the conversation, I mean 'up for it'. I definitely do not mean that the things the coachee wants to discuss need to be in perfect order in their mind before they start.

Naturally, we all experience times in life when we do not feel settled about and ready for what we are going to do, and we decide to just get on with it. At such times, it can work well to acknowledge that everything in the garden is not rosy, to say to ourselves that we will crack on anyway, make the best of it and see what unfolds.

If the coach is somewhat distracted or not feeling on top coaching form, they should take steps to address that situation, so that the conversation won't be compromised. The coachee will find the experience more useful if the coach is completely present, and this requires the coach to consciously choose to recognize and temporarily park the issues that might disrupt their coaching focus. The coachee should not end up with a mediocre session because the coach, for example, argued with their partner that morning and is busy stewing about that quarrel.

Coachees sometimes arrive for coaching feeling distracted, cross or otherwise unnerved. Their circumstances immediately beforehand may not have paved the way for clear or steady thinking. When this is the case, it is useful for the coach to explicitly check the coachee's readiness to engage in coaching. This inquiry also serves as an invitation for the coachee to set an intention to focus and make the most of the conversation. It may be appropriate to ask something like: 'How pre-occupied do you think you are going to be during this conversation?' It is a pertinent inquiry and should be asked in such a way as to avoid sounding impertinent.

In such a context, the ruffled coachee may respond that they do feel ready for the scheduled coaching, confirm that they are able to shift mindset and proceed as planned. In a situation where the coachee feels too stirred up to get straight on with coaching, we have a few options, including those described below. The chosen course of action can be decided on collaboratively between coachee and coach.

- The coachee could use some of the session to get things off their chest before then proceeding as planned. They could vent, talking through the edited highlights of the problem (not the whole nine seasons of the streamed drama) and then move on. If it seems fitting, the coach might remind the coachee how much time is available and ask: 'How much of this time do you think you will need to tell me enough for us to begin to do something about it?' (George et al., 2018).
- Occasionally, it is best to postpone the conversation and reschedule. This could mean resuming after a quick cup of tea (if time allows) or arranging to meet another time when the coachee can benefit more from the conversation. When this happens, the coach can reflect back sensitively what they are seeing, sensing and hearing to the coachee. Together, they need to make a plan for the coachee's next steps, with appropriate consideration of any safety and ethical issues.
- If the coach is suitably familiar with leading short grounding exercises, one of these may be helpful. For example, sitting quietly and inviting the coachee

to pay full attention to their in and out breath for a few minutes. This can have a surprisingly powerful effect that aids an emotional shift.

- The coachee may decide that the circumstances associated with their immediate stress or distraction should become the priority focus of the coaching conversation, trumping what they might have planned to discuss.
- Given how the coachee is feeling, re-contracting may be necessary as the conversation proceeds. I mean that the coachee, with the coach's support, may consciously revise the intended outcomes for the conversation. The process of deliberately re-contracting helps to prevent a situation where the discussion just slides off topic with little forward movement.

A favourite coaching question (to be asked in a sensitive way): 'How much of the session do you need to spend getting this off your chest before we move on?'

'Put on some shoes': starting where you are

Imagine for a moment that you are walking barefoot on a long path of searing hot sand, treading on thorns and sharp stones. An ancient Buddhist teaching declares that to avoid such a painful experience, you could decide to cover the whole path with leather.[2] Clearly, that is not a practical solution. A better idea would be to cover your feet with leather instead – that is, put on some shoes.

One interpretation of this metaphor is that we should focus on what we can control. Sometimes, people come to a coaching conversation wanting to do the equivalent of wrapping the world in leather to make things right for them as they walk on through their life. At the contracting stage and throughout the discussion, part of the coach's role is to help the coachee discern the external things which the coachee can influence. This is about helping them to find their shoes – so to speak – and to put them on and focus on where they can go immediately in the shoes. A coach assists the coachee to discover what they have the resources and willingness to do right now.

'Start where you are' is a statement of the obvious, yet it is not always such a straightforward thing to do. Lots of different things can prevent us from starting where we are. At the beginning of coaching, it is valuable for the coachee to look honestly at their current situation, warts and all. This assessment can involve acknowledging tough truths and feeling the weight of long carried emotional baggage. This kind of luggage is particularly well known to those of us working clinically in mental health settings.

Expectations can form part of that emotional baggage. Everyone (or almost everyone) is constantly swayed to some extent by expectations, be they those of others or those of ourselves. Without realizing it, coachees are often tempted to want to start, not where they are, but where they think they should already be – or where other people think they should already be. We all feel weighed down at times by expectations, making it harder for us to face up to our current position – that is, where we really are – and to move on from there. Coachees may feel drawn to focus on how they would start if the situation was like it used to be, or how they would start if the situation was how it would be if life was fair.

At the beginning of a coaching journey, coachees may be held back by a belief that they should have their proverbial ducks in a row before they can fully engage in the coaching process. But if we are always waiting until we have perfectly ordered ducks, we will be waiting all our lives. Starting where we are requires us to move forward with our motley ducks as they are. We have all procrastinated and kidded ourselves (cue the old joke about 'denial': not just a river in Egypt). We have all been in the position of waiting for certain conditions to be met before we start something: 'I'll cut the grass when the sun comes out', or 'I'll stop eating puddings after the holiday'.

It should be emphasized that when a coachee has a trusting alliance with a coach, this can bolster the coachee's capacity to see and start where they are. The tough truths and emotional baggage that I mentioned earlier can in fact contain valuable lessons and yield up tools for progress.

A favourite coaching question: 'What is in your power to change here?'

Now that we have explored the **C**, contracting stage of CLEAR, we will turn our focus to the **L**, listening stage. In other words, in Chapter 7 we will turn our attention to paying close attention.

Notes

1 In the field of positive psychology, *values* are seen as 'deeply rooted, abstract motivations that guide, justify or explain attitudes, norms, opinions and actions'. Values indicate 'what a person wants their life to stand for, what direction they want their life to go in and what will motivate them' (Green and Palmer, 2019).
2 Pema Chödrön is a Buddhist nun and author who has taught a great deal about her application of ancient wisdom to our modern lives. The Pema Chödrön Foundation. https://pemachodronfoundation.org/ (accessed 21 July 2021).

References

George, E., Iveson, C. and Ratner, H. (2018) *BRIEFER: A Solution Focused Practice Manual.* London: BRIEF.

Green, S. and Palmer, S. (eds.) (2019) *Positive Psychology Coaching in Practice.* Abingdon: Routledge.

Harris, R. (2009) *ACT Made Simple: An Easy-to-Read Primer on Acceptance and Commitment Therapy.* Oakland, CA: New Harbinger Publications.

7 L is for Listening: skills and knowledge

Introduction

Continuing with the **L** in CLEAR, we come to listening. The quality of our listening as coaches has an impact on the quality of our coachees' thinking. In this chapter, I consider how coaches listen actively and concentrate whole-heartedly on hearing their coachees. The chapter is divided into four sections.

In the first, I examine the power of silence. Sometimes silence can be more effective at yielding answers than even the best questions. A lack of spoken words does not equate to a shortage of communication.

The following section emphasizes the point that we do not just listen using our ears. We recruit our other senses and our intuition. Whilst it is not in a coach's remit to make speculative interpretations, it can be valuable for a coach to listen to what a coachee is not saying as well as to what they voice outloud.

Next, I claim that we can often be more effective coaches when we adopt an attitude of 'beginner's mind' and, as best we can, see with fresh eyes and listen with fresh ears. As humans, of course, we all have our biases (see Chapter 3). A coach's ability to listen properly can be hindered by assumptions about what a coachee brings.

The final section looks at stories, and how coaches listen to support coachees as they explore their narratives. The stories that coachees tell themselves about the world and how they fit in it, can be expressed and heard during coaching, and may be 'rewritten' in a valuable way as a result.

Listen is an anagram of silent

The place and use of silence in coaching cannot be overstated. An effective coach gives thought to how and when to constructively keep quiet and let silence do some important work.

Many of us fill silence out of habit. The extent to which we do so depends on numerous factors, including the situation, our mental state, and social and cultural considerations. At the end of a routine team meeting, I was chatting with a group of colleagues and asked them, 'Why do you think we speak?' They gave the following answers: we speak to inform, to show emotion, to bond, to be interesting, to be helpful, to support, to fix, to assert, to seem clever, to shut someone else up, to hurt, to control, to be liked, to break uncomfortable silence, and because we feel we can't help interrupting. In short, we speak for many reasons in the course of our day.

More often than we would like to notice or admit, in our everyday conversations we do not listen well because we are waiting to leap in when our conversation partner draws breath. We are often so determined to wedge our viewpoint into the discourse, that we only partially register what the other person is saying.

As coaches, when we are with someone who has become emotional, we may feel particularly under pressure to 'talk to fix'. Instead, it may be more useful for the person if we stay quietly by their side and remain open to the situation. We are still communicating with them when we do that. Such calm companionship in itself may be consoling, and it does not interfere if, in fact, their emotion is productive. It is possible that they are on the verge of what coach Susan Scott (2017) calls a 'nervous breakthrough'.

We need to remember when coaching that the main reason for the coach to speak is to promote and support the coachee's thinking. Gestures and brief utterances of encouragement by the coach are important and less likely to hijack the coachee's flow of thought than a verbal paragraph from the coach. A coach's stance of warm silence, saying nothing, or maybe just uttering one or two words, allows the coachee to listen to their own speech. Perhaps they will hear themselves in a new way.

A coachee called Leonie said, 'In coaching sessions, I can really hear myself think'. I will use conversations with Leonie to demonstrate the use of silence in coaching.

As Leonie's coach, I asked myself an important question silently throughout our conversations: 'Is what I want to say now going to be more useful to Leonie than if she continues to think in silence?'

To answer this question, I took my cues from Leonie. I noticed that if she was busy thinking, usually she would not be looking straight at me. Her eyes would tend to be directed slightly upwards and to the side: her head tilted sideways a little. She sometimes thought out-loud, saying her thoughts to herself, while I stayed out of the way. Leonie would re-establish eye contact when she was ready to return to direct conversation with me.

Even if remaining quiet feels uncomfortable, when we are coaching it is usually worth holding the silence just a little longer than we might in a run of the mill conversation. As Mark Twain apparently said, 'Never miss an opportunity to shut up'.[1]

Quiet, deep listening can be highly compassionate. At the risk of sounding corny, I will say that 'heard and heart' are words that share more than letters. Giving a coachee the gift of being both truly heard and deeply listened to can lead to a relief of suffering and also can help to free the person to be more honest with themselves. And when we are more honest with ourselves, we can become more accepting of ourselves and of others, and subsequently make authentic progress towards our goals.

Suggestion for you

During the next conversation you have, make a point of just noticing how you manage silences and create pauses. Play with holding silence longer and see what happens. Afterwards, ask the other person how it felt for them when you experimented with this.

Some people feel naturally at ease with silence. I used not to be one of them. But I have found that having a regular(-ish) meditation practice has helped me appreciate and maintain silence more than I used to. For example, I now choose consciously to drive the car and go about tasks at home with the radio off. By making these choices, my ease with silence has been boosted – as has my enjoyment of listening to the radio when I deliberately decide to. In our noisy, vocal world, silence can feel threatening or uncomfortable, and it really does not need to.

While attending carefully to the coachee, the coach cannot simultaneously plan their tea or think about what they should have said during a disagreement earlier in the day. If we find ourselves on that sort of track when we are coaching, we should stop, 'park it', and return our full attention to the conversation we are meant to be in.

A favourite coaching question: 'And …?'

Listening with more than our ears

Let's consider the word listening to mean paying attention. When we listen well, as the saying goes, 'we're all ears'. But we are not only ears. We can recruit our eyes, our hearts, our bodily sensations and our intuition to the listening process.

Sometimes, the words we hear as coaches in a coaching conversation may not correspond well with the messages we receive through our other senses. Michael, a coachee, says: 'I'm confident that my team is well on target with this month's clinical performance figures'. But his furrowed brow, slumped posture and averted gaze do not match his words.

In such a situation, the coach may decide to say they have noticed a mismatch between what Michael is saying and what he is conveying. Michael may or may not then conclude that what the coach noticed is relevant. What is important is that the coach reports what they have noticed without analysing or saying what they think it means. The coach might say, 'Michael, I notice the look on your face and how you're sitting don't seem to match the confidence of your words?'

Suggestion for you

During the next discussion or chat you have, if feasible, see if you can tune in to what you are feeling in your body as the conversation is happening. It might possibly enhance the communication rather than distract you from it.

We are equipped with some amazing and mysterious internal gadgetry, our intuition. Intuition refers to a capacity to understand something instinctively, without thinking it through in a conscious way. But we are wise not to rely too heavily on intuition. As is often the case for complicated gadgetry, we cannot assume it will always function with accuracy. When we are coaching, we can 'listen' to our hunches, but we should avoid any conviction that our own 'gut feeling' interpretation is the truth.

Sometimes what is not said by a coachee is as important as what is said. It can be useful in coaching to ask, 'What is it that you're not saying out loud?' The person may choose not to say 'it' out loud, or they may not know exactly what 'it' is. Yet the question may have served to raise awareness and nudge the coachee towards some clarity.

A favourite coaching question: 'What was it like to hear yourself saying that just now?'

Listening with a beginner's mind

In the beginner's mind there are many possibilities, in the expert's mind there are few.

– Shunryu Suzuki (1970: 21)

A small child toddles to the shoreline holding her dad's hand. It is her first ever visit to the seaside. She stands unsteadily on the wet sand as the sea water rushes up to surprise her little fat feet. The sun sparkles on the water and it is dazzling. This is all brand new to her. She had no prior conception this was in the world, and she has no idea what to expect. This little one experiences the seaside with an open beginner's mind, and her thoughts and senses are buzzing with fresh information and full of possibilities.

I am not suggesting that coaches listen as if they were toddlers on their first beach holiday, yet listening with a beginner's mind can be a valuable stance for a coach to take during some coaching conversations. When the coach listens in this way (we can call it beginner's mind listening), it can bring openness and curiosity to the conversation. This in turn supports the coachee to be more creative and optimistic.

Listening with a beginner's mind is likely to come naturally to us when we really are novices about the topic in question. It is not so straightforward in coaching when we know (or think we know) a lot about the coachee's context and the subject they are discussing. Beginner's mind listening is cultivated by learning to let go of our preconceptions. And we cannot do this well until we notice what they are.

Coaching supervision offers coaches the opportunity to reflect on their own biases and assumptions. These biases and assumptions can show up, and can risk tripping us up, in unanticipated ways when we are coaching.

Suggestion for you

Look around you and pick something up that is conveniently close by. (I have just grabbed a box of tissues.) Look at it with fresh eyes, for example from a different angle, study a detail that you have not registered before, or notice some quality about the object. Let your mind roam and imagine what un-thought of purpose it could be put to. What thoughts and feelings arise, and are any surprising?

I have just noticed that I relate to the tissue box as if it were a practical assistant – it offers up tissues freely to anyone close by who needs them.

Mental health practitioners in a coaching role may find it challenging to 'be' with beginner's mind. They have often spent many professional hours developing the ability to listen with an expert's mind, noticing patterns, interpreting those patterns in a certain way and then offering advice accordingly in line with professional guidelines. Beginner's mind is different to the mindsets that lead us to diagnose or reach firm conclusions. It can be harder than it might sound to notice our habitual judgements and our well-trodden thought paths.

Beginner's mind listening can lessen the likelihood that the coach will hinder the coachee's thinking by consciously or unconsciously guiding them in a certain direction.

A favourite coaching question: 'Is there anything obvious here that you are not actually noticing?'

Stories

Stories are key to the way we live. Humans are story-telling and story-hearing creatures. We link events, make patterns and evolve themes. Some of the narratives that we tell ourselves, or that others recount about us, hang around for years. These narratives influence our perception of the past and have a hand in shaping our future. They mould how we act, and can limit us or empower us.

Sometimes, we are emboldened by our personal storylines. At other times, they can stunt our ambition and keep us stuck. If one of your storylines is that you are a sporty sort of person, you would more than likely accept an invitation to join friends in a spontaneous game of rounders in the park without a second thought. Conversely, your personal story in relation to sport may be one of defeat and humiliation because many years ago at school you were often last in cross country races, returning bedraggled and mud-splattered. In that case, you are more likely to decline the invitation and so deprive yourself of the fun you could have had in that rounders game.

Suggestion for you

Reflect quietly for a moment: what are your personal storylines about the following:

- Sport and me?
- Maths and me?
- My feet?
- My boss?

The field of narrative coaching has been developed by David Drake (2017) and others, drawing on narrative therapy as a key source. Narrative coaching provides a boundaried opportunity for people to become familiar with their own stories and try out new ones that might serve them better. Coaching can help coachees re-write and re-tell the stories they hold onto about themselves and their life. There is opportunity for the updated stories to be rich in optimistic personal meaning and to be informed by personal values. Coachees can grow as a result.

It can be useful to edit and re-draft those stories as our lives progress. Let's illustrate this point with an analogy about gloves. We know that a pair of gloves that are perfect for a three-year-old boy will not fit him well when he is 12. But we do not need to totally discard our old stories: they can inform our new ones. In the case of the boy, he needs bigger gloves at age 12. But we know that what he learnt at age three – that gloves kept his hands warm – still applies.

With skilful listening, a coach can cultivate a coachee's awareness of their storylines. The coach can listen to the coachee's stories, not with a view to plunging into and advising about the content, but to prompt the coachee's realization of their own narratives. The coachee can come to see that their stories have been constructed in their mind and have an influence on their identity and behaviour, both at conscious and unconscious levels. The coachee can then begin to do things differently and see things differently. Stories can feel so much part of us that we do not realize they are just stories. We can benefit from viewing them for what they are, reviewing them and knowing they can be changed.

A favourite coaching question: 'As you hear yourself talk about this, are there any familiar patterns here for you?'

This chapter has focused on listening. Of course, the specific **L** stage in CLEAR is not the only part of a coaching conversation where great listening by the coach is called for. I will close this chapter with a coaching question used by the coach Nancy Kline (1999), who speaks and writes evocatively of 'Listening to ignite the human mind'.

What more do you think, or feel, or want to say?

This can serve as a key to unlock doors to productive thought by the coachee as the coach stays quiet and listens.

A simpler question with the same gist is also powerful: 'What else?'

Note

1   The quote is widely attributed to Mark Twain online, but I was unable to locate a verified source.

References

Drake, D.B. (2017) *Narrative Coaching: The Definitive Guide to Bringing New Stories to Life*, 2nd edition. Petaluma, CA: CNC Press.
Kline, N. (1999) *Time to Think: Listening to Ignite the Human Mind.* London: Ward Lock.
Scott, S. (2017) *Fierce Conversations: Achieving Success at Work and in Life, One Conversation at a Time.* London: Piatkus.
Suzuki, S. (1970) *Zen Mind, Beginner's Mind: Informal Talks on Zen Meditation and Practice.* New York: Weatherhill.

8 E is for Exploring: skills and knowledge

Introduction

Powerful coaching can transport a coachee on a voyage of discovery. They might seek new landscapes or view old ones through a new lens. This chapter and the next take us on a journey of coaching exploration.

There is a large area of terrain to cover. I begin by looking in greater detail at trust, which is a principal ingredient for valuable coaching. In addition, I examine the benefits for coachees of being unflinchingly open to the coaching process.

Next, I flag up that conversational exploration is more meaningful when it is guided by the compass of the coachee's core values. The coach can support a coachee to see clearly the values that matter to them most, and to craft plans to act in alignment with those values.

I then focus on the fact that human communication is peppered with metaphors. I argue that an awareness of the power and suppleness of metaphors enriches coaching conversations.

In the final section of this chapter, I suggest that humour has a role in coaching, provided it promotes connection and the coach retains a respectful attitude towards the coachee. A limp, insensitive or badly timed attempt at humour risks wrenching the rug from under the coach/coachee alliance.

Exploring and trust

For coaching to be truly effective, there needs to be trust between coach and coachee. Before a conversation moves on to exploration, the **C** (*contracting*) stage will have already addressed the more formal issues concerning confidentiality and boundaries.

One definition of trust is as follows: 'a firm belief in the reliability, truth or ability of someone or something'.[1] Trust can be subtle and rightly receives considerable attention in the training of most mental health service practitioners. Both coaches and coachees will almost certainly feel it in their bones when trust and rapport are lacking.

In her book, *Braving the Wilderness* (2017), Brené Brown uses the acronym BRAVING to describe important elements of trust. Box 8.1 contains a paraphrased summary of Brown's BRAVING.

Box 8.1: Paraphrased summary of the acronym BRAVING

B = Boundaries – we respect boundaries and ask for clarification if we are not clear

R = Reliability – we do what we say we will do

A = Accountability – we own up, apologize and try put it right when we have made mistakes

V = Vault – we do not share information or stories that are not our own to share; they are safe in the 'vault'

I = Integrity – we act according to our values rather than according to what seems easy, trouble-free or entertaining

N = Non-judgement – we are aware of our tendency to judge and so we practise talking about how we feel without being judgemental

G = Generosity – we give people the benefit of the doubt and interpret what others say and do in a generous light

---

I think that all coaches should be familiar with Brown's concept of BRAVING. It is a reminder that trusting others and trusting ourselves can be a courageous and vulnerable process.

A favourite coaching question: 'Is there anything else you want to ask so you're comfortable in this conversation?'

A trusting alliance with the coach can provide a psychologically secure setting for the coachee's exploration. John Bowlby (1988), psychologist, psychiatrist and psychoanalyst, wrote about how young children explore the world around them much more when they feel they have a secure base to return to. The concept does not apply only to children. We all feel more willing to venture into uncertain territory, and experience the vulnerability it can bring, if we do it from a safe context to which we can return.

In the safe space of a high trust coaching conversation, a coachee can loosen their grip on their existing ideas and assumptions and explore new possibilities and perspectives. When we allow our mind to leave its usual tracks (within reason), this can be an opportunity to learn surprising things. Sometimes in coaching, the discussion may begin in a relatively unpromising way. But if the coach and coachee trust in each other and have faith in the coaching process, then unexpected and rewarding consequences can unfold.

The following quick story is an example of 'letting go', and you will see how it perhaps parallels the way in which a coachee can let go in coaching. Gaping Gill is a deep pothole in North Yorkshire.[2] It is one of the largest known underground chambers in Britain. There is a smallish opening on the hillside which gives no clue at first look that it expands underground into a huge vault, with a volume similar to the size of York Minster, and a depth of over a hundred metres. On August Bank holidays, a local potholing club would set up a winch mechanism to lower willing members of the public, one at a time and for a small fee, right down into the pothole. Each visitor would sit in a little chair on a rope as they descended into the shaft.

I am not a particularly adventurous type when it comes to cliffs and caves, so I was rather surprised to find myself sitting in that chair. It was swinging gently on the rope in the mouth of the gill. Then the cavers started to lower me down. I descended through the dark, rocky shaft. It soon opened out and I discovered with exhilaration that I was just dangling in the roof space of this vast underground atrium. There were no walls within my reach to grab onto, no ground in contact with my feet, and no control over the rope suspending me.

In that situation, it was worth being brave and open to the possibility of making the most of a whole new view of things. A coaching conversation is far from a wet bank holiday trip down Gaping Gill. But an intention to be brave and to be open to possibility in a coaching session is a meaningful aim for both the coachee and the coach.

Generally, in life, we are inclined to hold tight onto the familiar. We like to feel we are standing on solid ground. Understandably, we prefer to feel secure. A coaching conversation can be a great opportunity to explore an idea or path that seems scary. Investigating that which scares us can increase our courage and wisdom, making us more open to opportunities we did not know we had.

The level of trust and sense of feeling comfortable in a coaching encounter is influenced by how the coach handles aspects of pace and timing. It is important for the coach to facilitate the best use of the available time while being careful to avoid a feeling of hurry or hassle. Coaches should maintain what Nancy Kline, in her book, *A Time To Think* (1999), calls a 'sense of ease'. A practical coaching approach can be summed up as 'not rushing, but getting a move on'.

Exploring and values

We all, I believe, should spend some time working out what really matters to us. Deep down, what do we want to get and give in life? What would we like to be remembered for after we are gone? Do our goals fit with our values? Are we on a path that is true to them? What needs to happen so that when we are on our death beds, we will know we have lived well?

The word 'values' can mean different things to different people. Put simply, our values describe how we want to behave on an ongoing basis: they are our 'chosen life directions' (Harris, 2009). A metaphor often used about values is that they are like a compass guiding our journey through life. So, we can set our compass and follow those bearings consciously. 'Values are intentional qualities that join together a string of moments into a meaningful path' (Hayes and Smith, 2005).

One way to help a coachee identify their values is for the coach to invite them to consider what is most important to them in relation to different aspects of their lives. In her book, *Practicing Happiness* (2014), Ruth Baer proposes the following categories (paraphrased below) for thinking about values:

- Values in our relationships
- Values in our work (including household and school)
- Values in our community (including local, further afield, environmental)
- Values relating to self-care, personal growth, recreation, leisure activity

Some values will belong in more than one of the above categories, or span all of them. For example, we may value compassion highly in all categories. Sometimes, we hold a value more dearly in one sphere of our life than another, such as valuing creativity especially in our leisure time if we paint.

The reality is that many of us are not consistently, consciously in touch with what is fundamentally important to us: at least, not in a thought-through way. Yes, we have goals and a sense of what is expected of us, but that is not necessarily the same as living by and acting on our values. When our goals are not in line with our true values, then we are less likely to achieve those goals. We are less motivated to strive for such aims when the going gets tough (which it invariably does at some point), and we probably will not feel satisfied even if we accomplish those objectives. Goals based on our values, by definition, will be the goals that mean most to us.

The coaching context can be a rewarding one in which to examine core values. As coaches, we hope coachees will undertake this exploration in a way that leads them to do more than just talk about their values. We want to support them to live their 'best' values too.[3]

It is feasible for coaches to ask coachees directly about their values, but 'What are your key values in life?' can come across as a rather abstract inquiry. It may evoke a response that is coloured by what the coachee thinks is expected of them, such as deciding they ought to say 'hard work'. Coachees may also find it difficult or may take a while to produce answers to such a broad question. There are other ways a coach can assist a coachee to explore their values.

Here are four possible routes that can lead a conversation deeper into values territory:

1 Suggesting: Choose a 'top five' from a values list
2 Asking: What are you doing when you are the best version of yourself?
3 Asking: What are you doing when you feel 'in the zone'?
4 Suggesting: Complete this sentence …

Let's consider each of these in turn.

Suggesting: Choosing a 'top five' from a values list. Asking the coachee to review a list of values can be a good starting place for a discussion.

The coachee is invited to pick the ten that mean most to them, then narrow the list down to their top five. A quick search on the internet reveals numerous versions of 'values cards' packs: these can be fun and useful as a coachee considers and picks their most important values.

Box 8.2: A list of some typical values

- achievement
- adventure
- authenticity
- beauty
- care for environment
- compassion
- contribution
- courage
- creativity
- curiosity
- determination
- fairness
- fame

- friendship
- growth
- happiness
- honesty
- humour
- independence
- kindness
- knowledge
- learning
- love
- loyalty
- openness
- optimism

- peace
- popularity
- purposeful work
- recognition
- respect
- responsibility
- security
- service
- spirituality
- trustworthiness
- wealth
- wisdom

Coachees may find it uncomfortable but illuminating to choose between values. One such case in point occurred when a coachee looked close to tears as he realized that he held core values in conflict with each other. He was upset as he acknowledged truthfully that his ambition at work mattered more to him than his relationship with his partner.

Asking: What are you doing when you are the best version of yourself? I expect that most of us enjoy thinking about our finest selves, and this involves connecting with our values and our strengths. When the coach asks the question, 'What are you doing when you are the best version of yourself?', or a variation of this question, this can lift the conversation. Asking the coachee about their 'best self' in relation to the subject under discussion can be particularly useful if the mood or energy of the session is flagging.

Coachees can usually recall times when their best version stepped up to face a challenge, care for others or respond wisely to a difficult situation. When they explore the elements of their best version behaviour, this may produce fresh insights or reinforce chosen values. Useful related questions are:

- 'What's the thing that you've done in the last two or three months that you're most proud of?'
- 'What are you most looking forward to doing in the next two or three months?'

Asking: What are you doing when you feel 'in the zone'? This question refers to the condition of 'flow' described by Mihály Csikszentmihalyi (2002). Flow can be summarized as a sense of deep absorption and focus, where we lose sense of time and feel at one with what we are doing. There is an easy propulsion about our activity in a flow state. This is the state when 'an individual feels completely satisfied through being absorbed in a task, even if the goal is not reached' (Falecki et al., 2019: 106).

As the coachee talks about times and pursuits during which they experience flow, they may realize more about the life directions they want to choose or change.

Suggestion for you

Thinking back to when you were a child, what did you do that totally absorbed you so that you lost track of time, or felt engrossed in something that seemed wonderful?

- What does that reflection lead you to think about how you're living your life now?
- Does that reflection lead you to any thoughts about your life's direction?

Asking a coachee about childhood experiences of being in the zone may help elicit answers that have ongoing relevance currently, and for the future. People often respond with genuine pleasure when asked such a question, but caution is required in relation to history of earlier life trauma.

Suggesting: Complete this sentence … People can bring their values into focus by considering their spontaneous responses when asked to complete sentences starting with, for example, the following words:

- People are …
- Happiness is …
- Love means …
- Money is …
- Work is …
- Family is …
- Success is …

This exercise is quoted from the relentlessly upbeat book, *The Art of Being Brilliant* (Cope and Whittaker, 2012).

Box 8.3 offers a few more questions that can help coachees to reflect on and tap into their values during a coaching conversation.

> **Box 8.3: More questions to help coachees reflect on their values**
>
> - Thinking of a recent time when you felt happy and uplifted, which of your values were being fulfilled?
> - Thinking of a recent time when you felt annoyed, which of your values were being denied or challenged?
> - When you are under pressure, which of your values do you tend to drop?
> - Who is your favourite character from a book or film and why?
> - What is your favourite animal and why?
> - What do you enjoy doing most at the weekend and why?
> - What do you enjoy most about your work and why?
> - Over the last few days or a week, what did you go out of your way to avoid?
> - Over the last few days or a week, what did you go out of your way to do?

People are often passionate about beliefs they cherish and espouse. In coaching conversations that focus on values, coachees can often make good progress when they hold their values powerfully in their heart, whilst also being able to think rationally about them. Coachees can then consider how best to put those values into action.

A favourite coaching question: What matters most to you in your life?

And how ever any of us might answer that question verbally, our real values are revealed by our behaviour. They are also shown by how we feel about our past behaviour, and by how we learn from it.

Exploring and metaphors

My understanding of a metaphor is that it is a word or phrase that we link to an action, object or feeling in a way that is not literally applicable, but is imaginatively applicable. For example, he is open-hearted, or she gave an icy stare.

When we take the time to think about it, we realize that hardly a sentence passes our lips without inclusion of a metaphor. We do not just talk in metaphorical language, that is how we think too. We all have our own metaphors and they are very much part of who we are. I believe that our thinking shapes the metaphors we use and the metaphors we use can shape our ongoing thinking.

> **Suggestion for you**
>
> See how many metaphors involving water you can think of off the top of your head (!) over the next couple of minutes.[4]

During a coaching conversation, the metaphors that work best for coachees are the ones they come up with themselves and which accurately represent situations for them personally. In the 1980s, counselling psychologist David Grove developed a way to lessen the chance of a coach's own metaphorical language muddying the waters of a coachee's thinking. This way of working is called the 'Clean Language' approach and involves asking 'clean', un-flowery questions to explore the coachee's perception and experience.[5] Clean questions include:

- What would you like to happen?
- And that's like what?
- And is there anything else about that?

'Less is more' with these so-called clean questions. The gist is that the coach keeps out of the way and asks the coachee to say more about the metaphors they choose to use. The coach's questions lack content and build on what the coachee has just said.

To see a Clean Language expert in action, you can watch Caitlin Walker online talking about her work (Walker, 2012).

Box 8.4: Clean questions example

When Tilda, a coachee, met for a coaching conversation with her coach, Rena, Tilda felt at home using metaphorical language to express herself.

Rena: What would you like to happen?
Tilda: I feel caught up, and I want to feel not caught up
Rena: And that's caught up like what?
Tilda: Like I'm caught up in a bramble hedge, and like I'm stuck and if I try to get out, I could get scratched and gouged.
Rena: And where do you feel caught up?
Tilda: I just feel sort of caught up all over.
Rena: And is there anything else about that?
Tilda: It's like I'm caught up and my clothes are getting snagged and I feel a bit panicky.
Rena: And when you feel caught up, what would you like to have happen?
Tilda: I'd like to have some really strong scissors in my hand so I could cut away the brambles. And I'd like to be wearing clothes that feel more protective so I'm better prepared. And I'd like to feel confident I could push through and get out of the other side of the hedge. And then, when I'd got through it, I'd look back at the hedge and say 'Right – we need to sort that hedge out – Cos I'm not going through that again!' But it's not just down to me to sort the hedge out, and wear protective clothes, there are other people who need to help with it.

Considering the above dialogue, it is evident that coachees may find themselves on a roll with their metaphors. Metaphors certainly seem to enhance some people's ability to reflect in a particularly personal way. We can see that rich material is yielded for the continuing coaching conversation. The coach does not need to understand it all. At the end of that kind of riff, it is worth the coach checking in with the coachee … 'So, where are we now?' This can prompt a summing up of meaning by the coachee about what has just happened.

The use of clean questions and metaphorical language is not, I think, a suitable way of coaching in all circumstances or with all coachees. People with very literal communication styles probably find this kind of approach less helpful.

A favourite coaching question: 'And that's like what?'

Exploring and humour

Let's talk about light-heartedness: it can pay to take it seriously in coaching. Appropriate and well-intentioned humour between the conversation partners holds a vital place in coaching. I am talking about vital in the sense of adding liveliness, as well as being important.

I am suggesting that when a coach uses considerate humour well, this has the power to help them connect with the coachee in a way that emphasizes warmth and can diffuse tension. Sharing a gentle laugh together is a collaborative process. The playfulness and curiosity often associated with humour can assist a coachee's creativity and exploration.

Sometimes, during a coaching conversation, a coachee may be surprised and amused about how their own thinking is developing. Or they may come to view an aspect of their situation as absurd or incongruous, and they point out the funny side. In such instances, naturally, coaches should employ sensitivity if they are invited to share the joke.

Misplaced flippancy, in coaching or other contexts, is often an unfortunate business and can rapidly derail trust. We all know that laughing with someone is different to laughing at them, but the distinction can seem a fine line: a coachee may perceive unpleasant mockery when none was intended. Coaches need to remain respectful and professional.

The coach, in addition to retaining awareness about how they themselves use humour, can fruitfully notice the coachee's use of it. For example, is it being used for avoidance? Humour can be employed (often unconsciously) to obfuscate or deflect. The coach may notice that whenever the conversation approaches a certain topic, the coachee makes light of the subject and then shifts the focus. If this is a clear pattern, it may be useful for the coach to mention that they notice this is happening. It can prove useful for such an observation to be respectfully mentioned out loud to the coachee, but it should be only that – an observation – not an interpretation of the behaviour.

Humour features in every culture. Coaches should give attention to possible cultural and social differences about what constitutes being amusing and what is taken to be rude. Although coach and coachee need to speak the same language, in everyday life terms, it is not always necessary for people to speak each other's languages to share something comical or subtly cheering.

The world of improvisational comedy has some useful lessons for coaches, and some coach training programmes include so-called 'improv work' for the following reasons:

- In improvisational comedy, a key principle is, 'Yes and ...'. Person one says something, and the next person to speak (person two) prefaces what they say with 'Yes and ...'. So, person two is required to acknowledge and build on what person one handed them regardless of whether person two likes it or not. 'Yes and ...' is a useful stance for coaching, and is in contrast to a 'No, but ...' type of response.
- In improvisational comedy, as in coaching, the ability to accurately tune in and pay attention is crucial.
- The action in improv keeps moving forward, thanks to the addition of sequential bits by the people involved, resulting in a finished piece of work. The same is often true in coaching.

Suggestion for you

So, I was getting into my car, and this bloke says to me, 'Can you give me a lift?'
  I said, 'Sure, ... You look great, the world's your oyster, go for it! '.[6]

- When reading this joke ... did you smile, did you groan or think 'what!'?
- Take a minute to reflect if, and how, you use humour in conversations.

With a focus on trust, values, metaphor and humour in this chapter, we have considered how coaches can support coachees to explore productively in coaching conversations. In Chapter 9, we will look further at the use of questions and challenge in coaching.

Notes

1 Oxford English Dictionary Online. https://www.oed.com/ (accessed 21 July 2021).
2 Gaping Gill. https://www.atlasobscura.com/places/gaping-gill (accessed 21 July 2021).
3 In capitalist cultures, there is an emphasis on working towards financial success. But if the acquisition of money is an all-encompassing value, and at the expense of social relationships, this has been linked to poorer well-being (Kasser and Ryan, 1993). Conversely, values associated with consideration for other people and the performance of acts of kindness correlate positively with happiness and well-being for those holding those values (Lyubomirsky, 2010).

4   Here are some possible answers to the metaphor exercise earlier in this section – a sprinkling of water metaphors:

> Like water off a duck's back
> Out of his depth
> Pour oil on troubled water
> Go with the flow
> Pour cold water on it
> In hot water
> Muddying the water
> Tidal wave of emotion
> Open the floodgates

5   The Clean Collection. https://cleanlanguage.co.uk/ (accessed 1 March 2021) – work of David Grove presented by Penny Tompkins, James Lawley and Marian Way.

6   Old Tommy Cooper joke. https://www.brainyquote.com/quotes/tommy_cooper_189065 (accessed 21 July 2021).

References

Baer, R.A. (2014) *Practising Happiness: How Mindfulness can Free You from Psychological Traps and Help You Build the Life You Want.* London: Robinson.

Bowlby, J. (1988) *A Secure Base.* London: Routledge.

Brown, B. (2017) *Braving the Wilderness.* London: Vermilion.

Cope, A. and Whittaker, A. (2012) *The Art of Being Brilliant: Transform Your Life by Doing What Works for You.* Chichester: Capstone.

Csikszentmihalyi, M. (2002) *Flow: The Classic Work on How to Achieve Happiness.* London: Rider.

Falecki, D., Leach, C. and Green, S. (2019) PERMA-powered coaching: Building foundations for a flourishing life, in S. Green and S. Palmer (eds.) *Positive Psychology Coaching in Practice.* Abingdon: Routledge.

Harris, R. (2009) *ACT Made Simple: An Easy-to-Read Primer on Acceptance and Commitment Therapy.* Oakland, CA: New Harbinger.

Hayes, S.C. and Smith, S. (2005) *Get Out of Your Mind and into Your Life: The New Acceptance and Commitment Therapy.* Oakland, CA: New Harbinger.

Kasser, T. and Ryan, R.M. (1993) A dark side of the American dream: correlates of financial success as a central life aspiration, *Journal of Personality and Social Psychology*, 65 (2): 410–22. https://doi.org/10.1037/0022-3514.65.2.410.

Kline, N. (1999) *Time to Think: Listening to Ignite the Human Mind.* London: Ward Lock.

Lyubomirsky, S. (2010) *The How of Happiness: A Practical Guide to Getting the Life You Want.* London: Piatkus.

Walker, C. (2012) TEDxMerseyside – Clean questions and metaphor models, *YouTube*, 11 February. https://www.youtube.com/watch?v=aVvcU5gG4KU (accessed 18 July 2021).

q E is for Exploring: more skills and knowledge

Introduction

In this chapter, I continue to show how coaches can support coachees to explore and expand their thinking during coaching conversations. The chapter is in four sections.

The first is about coaching questions. Naturally, questions prompt us to explore what we think, and the nature of our exploration depends on what we are asked and how it is put to us. On a good day, asking a good coaching question can feel like successfully tapping a security code into an automated door system. The correct code is entered and the door opens – that is, the question is asked and the coachee sees a way forward. But developing the skill and art of coaching inquiry involves more than knowing a particular combination.

In section two, I move on to stress that coaching falls short if it does not stretch the coachee. Effective push-back by the coach spurs the coachee's thinking and attention, encouraging them to extend themselves and develop.

I then emphasize that it can be illuminating for a coachee when the coach challenges them, in an empathic and robust way, to consider what they are assuming or avoiding. Coachees can then perhaps let go of assumptions which are limiting them, and confront their own patterns of avoidance.

The final section of the chapter brings some exploration themes together in the context of the ThinkOn® coaching approach.[1] The chapter concludes with a brief case study.

Exploring and questions

Coaching questions which strike the thinking jackpot are often short and straightforward. They are asked at the right time and in the right way, but on the understanding that there is never just one right way.

A distinction can be made between questions posed to broaden a coachee's thinking and those designed to focus their mind.[2] In the exploration phase of a coaching conversation, the usual emphasis is on broad thinking and the generation of ideas. This involves the use of an inquiry style that encourages the coachee to zoom out and think big. An exception is if the coachee wants to explore the details of a particular subject in depth, in which case the questions are aimed to help them zoom in and gain precise clarity. As we know, the right kind of questions are more likely to yield the right kind of answers. It is key for the coach to consider which type of question will best support the coachee to make good progress with their current thinking (zoom in or zoom out?).

Sometimes, a minimal question might suffice. Coachees may prefer to be left to think silently or even out loud with no interruption. Subtle inquiry by the coach can take the form of a facial expression or a single word uttered with upward inflection. A raised eyebrow, or a quiet yet emphatic 'Really??' can serve as penetrating questions.

Many coaches have a list of stock, 'off the peg' questions to hand. These can be a useful backup for the coach. One such question advocated by Michael Bungay Stanier (2016) is 'What's the real challenge here for you?' A coach can follow a logical progression in their line of questioning, using the so-called Cartesian Coordinates question stems (Deacon and Veale, 2010):

- **What will happen if you do** … for example … confront your colleague about the incident?
- **What won't happen if you do** confront your colleague about the incident?
- **What will happen if you don't** confront your colleague about the incident?
- **What won't happen if you don't** confront your colleague about the incident?

In answering these questions one by one, the coachee examines different angles of an issue in a systematic way.

Whilst there is value in stock questions, a fresh question carefully tailored to the moment usually fits the coachee's purpose better. Coaches need to remember that a question that worked brilliantly in one conversation may be fruitless in another.

Coaches ought to be aware of some potential pitfalls as they choose questions. The conversation is more effective if the coach avoids trying to be too clever: it is not all about the coach, even though as coaches we may occasionally be tempted to feel a bit proud of our approach. Long and elaborate questions from the coach can be disconcerting and annoying for a coachee. As coachees grapple with their own complicated thoughts, they need space to think, uncluttered by ornate questions from the coach.

Coaches can also ensure that coachees have space to think by asking one question at a time and 'letting it land': they should not shoot multiple questions in an almost machine gunfire fashion. They should also steer clear of asking pseudo-questions, which amount to advice superficially dressed up as a question. For example, 'Have you tried speaking to the manager and persuading her to …'.

Coaches sometimes get distracted in a coaching conversation as they try to devise a perfect question. If the coach gets caught up in pondering and formulating precisely what they will ask next, they can end up more than a few steps behind the coachee's thinking. If this happens, the question is best left unasked because it has passed its metaphorical use-by date. The coach needs to consign that question to what Claire Pedrick (2020) calls 'the golden bin bag'. The coach is better able to remain with the coachee's conversational flow if they are ready to make use of the golden bin bag.

Often, when I am listening carefully and feel fully attuned with what the coachee is saying, the right question seems to appear in my mind at about the same time that it starts to emerge from my mouth. This does not happen smoothly if I am not in close step with the coachee. I am sure that we have all experienced situations in our lives where words that tumbled out of our mouths would have proved less troublesome had they stayed in.

Great coaching questions often have the hallmarks shown in Box 9.1. I call these the 'Frequent 5 Ps of good coaching questions'.

Box 9.1: The Frequent 5 Ps of good coaching questions

Pithy
Pertinent
Powerful
Posed only when needed
Put one at a time

Exploring and challenge

As coaches, we can provide a more effective coaching conversation by presenting a degree of relevant and well-timed challenge for the coachee. Coaches need to provide some challenge for coachees to promote their awareness and progress.

If, at the start of a conversation, the coach asks the coachee for permission to challenge them during the meeting, this helps to set the scene. Occasionally, a coachee will say they do not feel up for much challenge in a particular conversation: the coach should respect that as a starting point.

If the coachee confirms that they are prepared for the coach to challenge them as the coaching process unfolds, it is likely that the coachee will anticipate some well-intentioned opposition from the coach. This anticipation may help to sharpen the coachee's thinking and keep them on their mettle.

To consider the intensity of challenge offered by a coach in a coaching conversation, think of the level of challenge as like a volume control on a device. One person's booming racket is another person's background noise. Metaphorically, then, the coach can turn the 'challenge volume' up or down to suit the situation as the conversation progresses.

John Blakey and Ian Day (2012) developed a valuable support/challenge model. Let us consider this model in relation to finding the right balance in coaching between providing support on the one hand and challenge on the other.

Blakey and Day describe how the level of challenge in a conversation can range from low to high. The level of support in that conversation can also range from low to high. This yields four scenarios (paraphrased below):

- *Low level of support and low level of challenge* from the coach: the coachee is at greater risk of developing and maintaining a 'can't be bothered' attitude.
- *High level of support and low level of challenge* from the coach: the coachee is not stretched, so the coaching is likely to be less than optimally effective.
- *Low level of support and high level of challenge* from the coach: the coachee may feel brow-beaten and might conclude the coach is just negatively on their case throughout the conversation. This is not an atmosphere conducive to constructive progress.
- *High level of support and high level of challenge* from the coach: when the coach strikes this balance well, the coachee can experience a sense of forward propulsion and energy.

Coaches can challenge coachees in a fruitful way when the spirit of collaboration is strong and trust is high. Some comedically sure-footed coaches employ an intentionally provocative style (Hollander, 2012), but this is tricky territory. This style involves the coach addressing the coachee with forceful but affectionate banter, contradiction and playing devil's advocate. To pull off such a method successfully, I would argue that the coach requires specific aptitude, and there needs to be a substantial degree of rapport between the conversational partners. When using a provocative approach, the coach also requires confidence in the coachee's current level of emotional robustness and also an awareness of relevant cultural factors.

As a general rule, I would advise coaches to exercise caution in using provocative techniques. But all coaches need to be willing to cross the line that separates comfortable and uncomfortable 'challenge territory' when required. Coaches ideally need to communicate with what Kim Scott (2017) calls 'radical candour'.

Scott's concept of radical candour means 'caring personally and challenging directly'. My understanding is that this model was developed for use in broader management and communication contexts, not specifically for coaching. Scott argues that trust and authentic communication are cultivated when the coach demonstrates well-attuned radical candour. This promotes respect and openness going both ways in the conversation.

Challenging assumption and avoidance

Questions that challenge assumptions and which seek to highlight areas that are being avoided (consciously or unconsciously) are important in the **E** (*exploring*) stage of a CLEAR conversation and throughout it more broadly.

The extent to which such questions are perceived as challenging by the coachee depends on the context and the relationship.

Let's think about inquiring into a coachee's assumptions, bearing in mind that some of a person's assumptions will be more accurate than others. Some will serve a helpful purpose for the coachee, or may have done so in the past. Other assumptions cause trouble from the moment they are formed.

Our minds naturally fill in the gaps when we hear a story that lacks information (Segal et al., 2018). Box 9.2 demonstrates this.

Box 9.2: Our minds naturally fill in the gaps when we hear a story that lacks information

Now, quickly cover the next four lines with your hand, then move your hand to read one line at a time.

- John was on his way to school.
- He was worried about the math lesson.
- He was not sure he could control the class again today.
- It was not part of a janitor's duty.

Did you make assumptions? That is, assuming you have not read about John before!

As I discussed in Chapter 7, we all shape our perceptions and memories to fit with our narratives and this involves assumptions that often go unchallenged. It is all too possible for our accepted assumptions to become rocks on the track to our goals.

Whilst some assumptions are short-lived, we have carried others with us for a long time and they underlie or are linked to the stories we tell ourselves. Sometimes, coachees can uncover and investigate some of their own suppositions relatively easily with the coach's help. Other assumptions are well camouflaged, and they are more tethered in coachees' minds or less accessible.

Here are some examples of coaching questions to flush out and challenge assumptions:

- What assumptions are you making that it would be useful to challenge? (note, the coach is making an assumption about the presence of assumptions)
- What assumptions are you making that might be holding you back?
- What would have to be true for your assumption to be right?
- What would have to be true for your assumption to be wrong?
- How do you feel about checking out this assumption?
- How will you check it out?
- What will it mean if you stop assuming 'x'?
- What will it mean if you continue assuming 'x'?

Coaches often encounter a situation where a coachee assumes that their choice or way forward involves *either* action 'a' *or* action 'b'. An option might exist, however, for some combination of 'a and b'. This combination might end up being a potential action 'c' which the coachee had not considered.

Coaches can assist coachees to challenge assumptions, and in so doing invite them to seek new perspectives. The same situation can be seen from a variety of standpoints associated with different assumptions, as Box 9.3 demonstrates – albeit in an oversimplified way to make a point.[3]

Box 9.3: Same event, different perspectives and assumptions

Same event	Different perspective/assumptions
Polly treads in dog muck	Oh, stupid me as usual!
Pallab treads in dog muck	Oh, what a selfish dog owner!
Pia treads in dog muck	Oh, harmful germs all over my shoes!
Paula treads in dog muck	Oh, I knew I was right (as usual) not to wear sandals today!

I will now move on to consider the subject of how coachees sometimes shun areas it would be useful for them to think about. We all tend to do this to some extent, and when we do, we risk not facing up to important considerations in our lives (or whatever aspect of them is under discussion). Coaching can help us face the music, and good coaches support coachees to examine areas they might be unhelpfully avoiding.

Many years ago, as a junior doctor, I had fortnightly meetings with a wise and rather formidable supervisor who was a psychoanalyst. At every meeting she would skewer me with her gaze and say: 'And what are you running from?'

When I am coaching, I am not acting as a supervisor or posing as a psychoanalyst: I do not direct that particular query to coachees. But sometimes in my mind, I can almost hear the richly accented voice of my old boss urging me to ask a version of it.

When a coachee has explored and acknowledged what they are reluctant to face, they can then consider more clearly what they want to do about it. Questions to explore a coachee's avoidance can range from the obvious (i.e. 'What are you avoiding?') to variants such as:

- 'What are you pretending not to know?'
- 'How would you explore this issue if you were being really brave?'
- 'What do you least want me to ask about this?'
- 'What is it about this that you're not saying out loud?'

Favourite coaching question: What aren't you saying out loud?

Before leaving the subject of how coaching can prompt coachees to explore areas they may be avoiding, I will mention a non-sweary version of an apt quote by Susan Scott (2017): 'The truth will set you free – but first it may thoroughly irritate you'.

Exploring and ThinkOn®

The ThinkOn approach to coaching involves useful elements that can enhance the exploration stage of a coaching conversation.

I will remind you here of the ThinkOn Key Thinking Principles (Gilbert and Chakravorty, 2015) (see Chapter 5). These are common foundations for successfully making a difference, and are as follows:

1 Have a **strong reason why** you want to make a difference
2 **Define your goal** before starting to make a difference
3 **Consider possibilities** and **plan your priorities** before taking action
4 Have **self-belief** that you can and will make a difference
5 **Involve others** to help you make a difference
6 **Take personal responsibility** for your actions
7 **Take action** and measure the results of the difference you make

A ThinkOn technique called the Thinking Effectiveness Framework[4] helps us to examine and categorize our thoughts about an issue, and to consider the impact that those thoughts have on us. The coach invites the coachee to explore their ideas about the issue in some or all of the following ways:

- What statements come to mind for you? (in relation to this issue)
- What questions come to mind for you? (in relation to this issue)
- What recollections come to mind for you? (in relation to this issue)
- What ideas for the imagined future come to mind for you? (in relation to this issue)

Delving into the subject in this systematic way, the coachee can more clearly identify their helpful and hindering thoughts about it. With awareness of the need for progress, they can make choices about how they will respond to their helpful and hindering thoughts.

When we work with a coachee to explore possible ways in which they might work towards the achievement of a goal, we can invite them to consider the following areas:

- What actions and resources might be required to achieve a goal?
- How can the involvement of other people contribute to the achievement of a goal?

- How might those other people benefit too?
- What are the things that might prevent a goal from being achieved?

Before we conclude this chapter, I will describe aspects of a case study. This showcases use of some ThinkOn Key Thinking Principles, employed at the exploration stage of a coaching conversation (goals having been clarified initially).

Case study: Aran

Aran has recently recovered from a prolonged period of low mood. Most of his old optimism has come back, and he has decided to return to his university studies. However, he knows this will involve some real challenges. In coaching, he wants to explore the issue of what he calls, 'a successful return to university'.

Before going on to explore this subject, the first step is for Aran to gain some clarity about what a 'successful return to university' would look like for him. He sums this up as firstly, keeping up with his studies and, secondly, continuing to feel 'happy enough overall' (whilst acknowledging that no-one is happy all the time). So, Aran has identified two strands to his overall aim. The strands are related to each other, and Aran and the coach decide it is preferable to consider them separately to start off with. Aran chooses to focus first on thinking about how he can keep up with his studies.

The coach can help Aran to explore this area constructively by asking questions about what he might need to do to achieve the goal, how others might be involved and what might get in the way of a successful outcome. During this process, it is useful for Aran to jot down some notes to capture his key thoughts.

First, the coach invites Aran to be more specific about the phrase 'keeping up with studies', and to identify what tasks he will need to complete in order to do this, for example, establishing a feasible timetable and routine. Then the coach can also prompt him to consider what resources he will need, such as equipment and a suitable place to study.

Next, the focus moves to assisting Aran to think about how others may have a role in supporting him to keep up with his studies. Who might lend a hand? How might he involve them? How might they help? How might he reciprocate? For example, friends, tutors, family members and student support staff could reinforce his efforts.

In addition, Aran needs to give attention to potential obstacles and risks associated with his aim to keep up with his studies, like erratic sleep patterns. Once these are 'out in the open', he can think how he might overcome obstacles, minimize risks and weigh up any implications. The coach can support Aran's exploratory thinking further by asking him to contemplate any assumptions he is making about the situation or any limitations he may have imposed on himself.

Following this exploration and consideration of possibilities, the conversation can then progress to the next stage. This will go on to chart Aran's chosen action plan in relation to this part of his goal – that is, what he will actually do, having examined a range of options, to keep up successfully with his studies. Aran's coaching journey has the potential to strengthen his sense of hope and personal agency and his awareness of his opportunities.

The next two chapters look at coaching skills especially useful for the later part of a CLEAR coaching conversation which focuses on action and review, **AR**. When we reach the *action and review stage*, the coaching ceases to be so much about generating possibilities, and more about prioritizing, planning and summing up.

Notes

1 Go M.A.D. Thinking. https://gomadthinking.com/ (accessed 21 July 2021).
2 The ThinkOn® model describes these as 'The two types of high-quality questions'.
3 Box 9.3 involves adaptation (with a change of meaning and emphasis) of a story used in the field of cognitive behaviour therapy (Stott et al., 2010).
4 The Go M.A.D. Thinking System. https://gomadthinking.com/the-go-m-a-d-thinking-system/ (accessed 21 July 2021).

References

Blakey, J. and Day, I. (2012) *Challenging Coaching: Going Beyond Traditional Coaching to Face the FACTS*. London: Nicholas Brealey.

Bungay Stanier, M. (2016) *The Coaching Habit*. Toronto: Box of Crayons Press.

Deacon, M. and Veale, R. (2010) *GROW Coaching Model Cards – Advanced* (Reveal More Coaching Cards). Gloucester: Reveal Solutions. https://www.revealsolutions.co.uk/coaching-cards-courses-books-resources/grow-coaching-model-cards-advanced/.

Gilbert, A. and Chakravorty, I. (2015) *Solution Focused Coaching*. Woodhouse Eaves: ThinkOn Books.

Hollander, J. (2012) *Provocative Coaching: Making Things Better by Making Them Worse*. Bancyfelin: Crown House Publishing.

Pedrick, C. (2020) *Simplifying Coaching: How to Have More Transformational Conversations by Doing Less*. London: Open University Press.

Scott, K. (2017) *Radical Candor: How to Get What You Want by Saying What You Mean*. London: Macmillan.

Scott, S. (2017) *Fierce Conversations: Achieving Success at Work and in Life, One Conversation at a Time*. London: Piatkus.

Segal, Z.V., Williams, M. and Teasdale, J. (2018) *Mindfulness-Based Cognitive Therapy for Depression*, 2nd edition. New York: Guilford Press.

Stott, R., Mansell, W., Salkovskis P. et al. (2010) *Oxford Guide to Metaphors in CBT: Building Cognitive Bridges*. Oxford: Oxford University Press.

10 Action (A) and Review (R): skills and knowledge for supporting next steps and closing well

Introduction

This chapter and the next take us to the action and review parts of the CLEAR model. The skills and knowledge presented here are especially important in the later stages of a coaching conversation.

In the **AR** (*action and review*) stages, the coach helps the coachee to focus on what they have learnt during the coaching encounter, to plan what they will do next and to consider how they will review subsequent progress. The different threads of the preceding exploration (**E** stage of CLEAR) are drawn in and tied together. The **AR** stages can result in a ready-to-go action plan and/or may produce important concluding reflections for the coachee.

In this chapter, I address three related themes, each with its own section. In the first, I focus on how the coach can manage the situation when it feels like a coaching conversation has become stuck. The coach can take steps to help to 'unstick' it, and to free up the coachee's thinking.

I then move on to consider the level of anticipated struggle for the coachee if they were to go ahead with their evolving action plan. In other words, will implementing the plan be too challenging for the coachee or maybe it is not ambitious enough? The most effective action plans usually involve some struggle and stretch for the coachee – but not too much. With the coach's help, coachees can discover a balanced approach while deciding their course of action.

The final section explores how coaches support coachees to think constructively about obstacles they may face as they execute their action plan. This section also highlights that it is sometimes possible for coachees to re-frame past mistakes and failures, and develop more encouraging perspectives on them.

Stuck

It is not that unusual in a coaching style conversation or coaching session to reach a point where progress has stalled: the coachee feels stuck and the coach does too. At such times, it is important for the coach to have faith in the coaching process and to trust the resourcefulness of the coachee to find a way forward. Sometimes being stuck can lead to unexpected learning or significant shifts for the coachee. This is more likely if the coach holds their nerve and avoids leaping in to try to rescue and forcefully unblock the situation.

The coach might name the situation: *Are we stuck?*

If the coachee agrees that they are stuck, the coach can go on to say:

- So, what do we need to do now to make the remaining x minutes as useful as possible for you? *or*
- So, what do we need to do to unstick this? *or*
- So, which bit of the conversation seems to be most stuck for you?

There are times when it is helpful to have a break. Usually though, a constructive way forward can be found without the need for this. If the coachee's thinking is not flowing well when seated during the conversation, it might be worthwhile to try something different. Options include:

1 Continuing to talk while standing or walking.
2 Moving the chairs or swapping seats around (or something similar). During one coaching conversation, the coachee, Adam, felt stuck. He opted to continue the conversation sitting under a large table. Adam suggested that while he sat on the floor, the coach should remain in their chair. Adam said he could think better sitting there, and he also seemed to prefer the lack of eye contact. It was an unusual arrangement, but it seemed to work quite well. He made some useful realizations and developed an action plan under the table.
3 Inviting the coachee to draw, write in coloured pens or make diagrams can be helpful to stimulate fresh thinking if spoken words do not hit the spot.
4 Using so-called props to facilitate thought, expression and planning might seem a bit odd to some coachees at first. For others, it is second nature for them to grab items from their immediate surroundings and use them to represent the things and the relationships they are thinking and talking about. When I am coaching face-to-face, I often have a pot of buttons in my bag (mixed colours, shapes, textures, and sizes). I sometimes offer the coachee the option to tip these out and use them to 'make' a bit of their world. This activity can be a flop or a success, or something in between – the coach will have an idea of the coachees to whom it would appeal. Occasionally, doing this, coachees can become very engrossed and attribute considerable meaning to the buttons they choose and where they place them. If this happens,

the coach should keep out of the way. The coach might comment on what they notice, but should avoid interpretation. That is for the coachee to do. This activity may seem like playing, but think how much children learn from play: adults can too.

Solution-focused brief therapy has provided lines of questioning that are valuable in coaching conversations (Iveson et al., 2012), particularly when a coachee feels stuck. These questions include so-called 'exception questions' and 'coping questions'. Exception questions may be useful if a coachee focuses excessively on a problem situation, and coping questions can bolster resourcefulness. Given the tendency of the human mind to be like a Teflon surface to positive experience and like Velcro to negative experience, it is important for coaches to be familiar with exception questions and coping questions.

Examples of exception questions:

- Can you think of some point in the past month when this was not a problem?
- So, when is this not a problem?
- When it's not a problem, what's happening instead?
- What's different about the times when it isn't a problem?
- What's different about you when it isn't a problem?

Examples of coping questions:

- How are you managing to stop this getting worse?
- What helps you most with this?
- Who helps you most with this?
- What do they do to help?
- What would you advise someone with this problem to do?

The words we use inside our own heads and out loud when we feel stuck also influence our capacity to become unstuck. The word 'but' demonstrates this point. When we use 'but' in our dialogues with ourselves or others, it can wield surprising power for such a little word (Scott, 2017).

Hearing 'but' in a two-part sentence often leads people to assume that the second part of the sentence diminishes or negates the first part. The word 'but' can imply an uphill or stuck feeling. 'But' might also come over as critical or provocative if the person who hears it is feeling sensitive at the time. This might seem precious, but it happens frequently. Here is an example:

- 'You've worked hard but there's a lot left to do'
  could be heard as:
  'There's a daunting amount left to tackle'
  or even:

'You've not worked hard enough'
as compared to:

* 'You've worked hard and there's a lot left to do'.
  which seems more to be a plain statement of two facts.

Suggestion for you

Try saying 'and' instead of 'but' in your thoughts and in conversations with people (unless you really do mean 'but').

How much struggle?

Let's think about the concept of 'struggle' in the context of a coachee mapping out their next steps in a coaching conversation. When we exert ourselves constructively to achieve a meaningful and realistic goal, we feel stretched and squeezed at times. Often, we need to strive hard to achieve our aims and tough, productive toil certainly has its place.

Productive toil is clearly not the same as futile struggle, however. Futile struggling involves wasting a great deal of mental and physical energy, battling on blindly in vain to achieve something that is objectively out of reach, and pursuing 'flying pig outcomes' (i.e. outcomes as likely to happen as pigs are to fly).

We can use a metaphor here drawn from acceptance and commitment therapy. It is called 'Tug of war with a monster' (Harris, 2009). Imagine you are in a tug of war with an enormous, extremely strong monster. You have got one end of the rope and the monster has the other, and in between you there is a deep, dark pit. At first, you think that the best thing you can do in that situation is to pull your end of the rope really hard. But, of course, the huge monster just pulls back harder. An alternative course of action for you would be to drop the rope. You could then go off to do something more constructive that is within your control and that will not result in you tumbling into a pit.

The relevance to a coaching situation is that the coachee should believe that they are setting out on an action plan that is possible, in large measure, for them to complete. In previous chapters, we discussed the need for the coachee to set goals that are relevant and feasible. At this stage in the coaching conversation, the coachee needs to develop an action plan made up of suitable and manageable steps. However, as seen in Chapter 8 in the section on values, there is a place for aspiration. An action plan may have a focus on maintaining a direction of travel determined by values rather than reaching an ultimate end-point.

During the exploration stage of the CLEAR process, the coachee may have generated multiple possible actions that they potentially could pursue. In the action/review part of the conversation, the coachee now needs to decide what they actually intend to do, choosing from the options they have generated. The process of making these choices and distinctions involves, amongst other things, the coachee identifying which of those elements they can best influence or control.

When developing or reviewing action plans the coachee, with the coach's support, should aim to:

- Be aware of what they can and what they cannot control (even if this requires facing up to uncomfortable truths)
- Let go of attempting to control the things they cannot control (even if this is hard)
- Focus action plans on what they can control (so conserving their energy and lessening frustration)

Coaching questions which reflect these points are:

- Which part of this situation do you have most control over?
- How does having control over that affect your action plan?
- Which part of this situation is beyond your control?
- How does lacking control over that part affect your action plan?

A favourite coaching question: What part of this situation can you influence/control the most?

Rocks, tripwires, failures and mistakes

Here, I look at how coaching can help coachees to see and manage potential obstacles to their plans, and also how coaching can support coachees to move on after they have erred or experienced failure.

It makes good sense for coachees to consider what might scupper their action plans, trip them up or hold them back on the road to achieving their goals. Sometimes they can see the potential problems ahead, the rocks, and sometimes they cannot. The ones they cannot foresee are the tripwires. Coachees can then think about strategies that will help them to cope with or overcome obstacles.

There are good reasons for a coach and coachee to explore the subject of rocks and tripwires in relation to a coachee's plans, including:

- Anticipating particular bumps or rocks in the road can help us to cope with those bumps better when we come to them
- Thinking about potential obstacles enables us to prevent or avoid some of them
- Being realistic about the fact that there will also be unforeseen hindrances encourages us to cultivate a flexible attitude and – to mix my metaphors – be better at rolling with the punches.

Naturally, we cannot always foresee or prevent problems, but we can work on developing a mindset that helps us to respond wisely and adaptively as obstacles occur. I think that one of the best ways to foster such a mindset is to get into the habit of noticing what we think and how we behave when we meet the small, everyday obstacles we encounter in daily life. I have heard these little difficulties referred to as 'bourgeois suffering' (Chodron, 2007). For example, what do you think and how do you behave when a big, flash car, with a nonchalant driver, swings into the recently vacated parking space you had been patiently waiting for? Or when you asked very politely for a medium decaf latte and a large caffeinated cappuccino is thrust at you by a peevish barista?

These are examples of bourgeois suffering, but they are also an opportunity. We can reflect on our responses and learn from them. Coaching conversations can be a good place for some of this reflection and learning to take place.

Suggestion for you

Next time you encounter some of your own bourgeois suffering, notice your thoughts and how you behave. Maybe practise a flexible, tolerant mindset?

The coachee should also consider how they will respond when the going gets gruelling as they put their plans into action. Where will they draw strength from at those times? And who will help them?

Some people like to consider in advance what they will say to themselves to feel galvanized if they falter: for example, 'No-one said this would be easy – dig deep and keep on going'. I was working for important exams at a time when an energizing and earwormy song by Billy Ocean was popular. The opening lines go: 'When the going gets tough, the tough get going'.[2] It may seem trivial that often I used to hum the first few lines to motivate myself to revise, but I admit that humming them can still cheer me on all these years later.

Another strategy that the coach could suggest is that the coachee writes a self-addressed letter of encouragement to be read when they hit a rough patch in their journey reminding them of:

- the reason for taking this path and why it matters
- their personal strengths that will help them achieve the goal
- the anticipated rewards of achieving the goal
- the potential costs of not achieving it and what is at stake

But obstacles are not necessarily bad news. They can make the journey more interesting, keep us on our toes and teach us unexpected lessons. We can all think of times in our lives when we faced circumstances that we had not wished for and that felt extremely taxing at the time. Those episodes will have probably taught us valuable lessons about ourselves and the world as long as we were, or are, ready to learn them.

Here is a brief example from my own experience. Obviously, we all know that we are going to die. But when I was seriously ill, unsurprisingly the prospect of my own death felt closer at hand. At that time, I realized that there were aspects of everyday life that I had hitherto not properly appreciated, and others about which I had needlessly worried or grumbled. I concluded that I did not have time to harbour numerous unnecessary worries or little gripes. That was a useful lesson that I have not forgotten (although I admit to still worrying and griping ... just less than I used to).

I want to raise a paradoxical point. Occasionally, those personal characteristics that we generally regard as our strengths can make obstacles more difficult to overcome. If our strengths are not 'diluted', they can morph into weaknesses. For example, perseverance can be a great character asset, but 'undiluted' it might cross the line into stubbornness. Flexibility is wonderful, but in excess may manifest as dithering. A stubborn approach or a dithering attitude towards obstacles can mean they become almost insurmountable.

Sometimes, we see the rocks as more of a problem than they need be, or we cannot see beyond them at all. When a coachee finds him or herself in this situation, the coach's questions may help the coachee see things more objectively or optimistically. Such questions might be around the areas familiar to us from earlier in this book, such as assumptions, avoidance and establishing which aspects are in the coachee's control. We all have minds that make mountains out of molehills[1] at some point, and some people's minds make a lot of mountains. This propensity may be holding them back and coaching can provide them an opportunity to challenge it.

A favourite coaching question: What might get in the way of your plan?

Let's move on to shine a light on how we might regard failures and mistakes in a coaching situation. The reality is, we all make mistakes and experience some failures. They, too, can provide rich teaching if we are willing to tolerate the vulnerability and discomfort that this learning can involve. The aftermath of mistakes and failures can be fertile ground in which we can sow seeds for a better future.

I am not, however, denying that misfortunes and blunders sometimes have grim and lasting consequences. No amount of positive perspective will erase the reality that they occurred. Coaches can assist coachees to find a way forward whereby they acknowledge the realities but do not feel routed by them.

So, during the course of coaching conversations, coachees can contemplate past mistakes constructively and consider how to avoid future missteps. Occasionally, they may also realize as coaching proceeds that, in the context of their current actions or life choices, they are in the process now of making a momentous mistake. In such a situation, the coach has a role in supporting the coachee to deliberate steadily on what to do next.

This steady deliberation is important. Quite often in life, when we realize we have made a mistake or have gone wrong, our reactions make things worse, like someone throwing water on a chip pan fire. The coach can support the coachee to resist the reflex pull of a hasty and ill-thought through plan, and instead approach next steps more calmly. You will probably have seen old films where unfortunate cowboys or villains find themselves in treacherous quicksand. Those that thrash about violently are quickly sucked to their doom below the muddy surface. The ones who will live to tell the tale move steadily in the quicksand, keep their heads up and assess their surroundings for available resources. That sort of approach can be useful in everyday life as well as in quicksand.

Here we will give more attention to failure: coaching conversations are a particularly good place for constructive inquiry when the coachee uses the F-word. The coach can help the coachee focus on the development of innovative and workable plans, while taking into account the lessons learnt from what did not work previously. The acknowledgement of what has not been done well means facing the situation with open eyes when the preference might instead be to shut them. It does not need to involve either excessive self-recrimination or blame of others. Some coachees may overemphasize their own contribution to a failure scenario or mistake, and some may tend to attribute all the fault elsewhere. When the coachee reflects in response to the following coaching questions, a fresh perspective and some clarity may emerge to inform the coachee's forward progress.

- What part did your actions play in this going wrong?
- Now that you've said that, what does it mean for what you will do next?
- What do you know now that you didn't know before (X happened)?
- What does that mean in relation to what you'll do next?

My mum used to say, 'Sometimes things have to go wrong before they can go right', and there is some value in seeing life like that. Often, we can go a long way to putting right what has gone wrong, and often we will do better next time. 'Fall seven times and stand up eight', states a Japanese proverb. A coach can play a useful role as a coachee decides to get to their proverbial feet again for the eighth time.

Chapter 11 offers further suggestions for coaches at the **AR** stage of CLEAR as they work with coachees to bring the conversation to a close, summing up insights and setting out intentions.

Notes

1   However, it is worth being vigilant for molehills, both figurative ones and real ones: apparently, William III of England died from his injuries after the horse he was riding tripped on a molehill, fell and crushed him.
2   Billy Ocean – 'When the Going Gets Tough, the Tough Get Going' (in London 1986) [music video]. https://www.billyocean.com/videos/ (accessed 21 July 2021).

References

Chodron, P. (2007) *No Time to Lose: A Timely Guide to the Way of the Bodhisattva.* London: Shambala.

Harris, R. (2009) *ACT Made Simple: An Easy-to-Read Primer on Acceptance and Commitment Therapy.* Oakland, CA: New Harbinger Publications.

Iveson, C., George, E. and Ratner, H. (2012) *Brief Coaching: A Solution Focused Approach.* London: Routledge.

Scott, S. (2017) *Fierce Conversations: Achieving Success at Work and in Life, One Conversation at a Time.* London: Piatkus.

11 More about A and R: skills and knowledge for supporting next steps and closing well

Introduction

This chapter continues with coaching guidance particularly useful for the **AR** (*action and review*) stages of CLEAR. I examine five areas for coaches to consider, presented in five sections.

In the first, I emphasize that it is important for both the coach and the coachee to be clear about the coach's role as action plans are being honed. A coachee may be aware that the coach has experience of the subject under discussion and may ask for the coach's suggestions about how to proceed. How should the coach respond?

I then argue that it is often useful for a coachee to view their situation from some metaphorical distance when they are working out next steps. I suggest how this broader kind of observation can be achieved by looking ahead into the imagined future, or by adopting the hypothetical perspective of someone else.

In the third section, I focus on the salience for coachees of prioritizing and sometimes even reflecting on 'What is the one thing …?', when it comes to designing and implementing successful plans. Invariably, when we prioritize something, we downgrade the importance of something else. Coaches can support coachees to set priorities in a particular area of life, such as at work. As they do this, coachees should not lose sight of their life's big picture and the value of a so-called balanced life, involving a personally suitable mix of activities.

Next, I explore the theme of responsibility in relation to the plans that coachees develop during the **AR** part of coaching conversations. Here, I suggest that if a coachee develops an action plan, they need to be clear they will, in fact, act on it. The metrics chosen to measure the success of any action plans need to be appropriate to the goal and to be attainable.

The chapter closes with a focus on how coaches can help coachees to finish off the coaching conversation well, consolidating the benefits of the coaching and with the scene set for what will come next.

Different hats

When we go about our different roles in life, we are wearing different meta-phorical hats. It is usually sensible to wear only one hat at a time. In coaching conversations, the coach and the coachee should both be clear which hat the coach is wearing. For most of the conversation, they will of course have on their coach hat. This means that they abide by the coaching basics of 'asking not telling', active listening and other aspects of coaching we have covered in depth in this book.

A coach using a strictly pure coaching method would not offer advice. However, some coaches take a more flexible stance, particularly during this **AR** phase of the CLEAR conversation. Sometimes the coachee asks the coach's advice. Occasionally, the coach may think that it would be useful or necessary to step out of coach role, for example, if the coach thinks the coachee should seek additional professional help.

If a coach would like to provide a suggestion during a coaching conversation, the usual practice is for them to first seek permission from the coachee. The coach's suggestion is kept brief and after offering it, the coach stops talking and continues listening. Say that the coachee asks for the coach's ideas about tackling some tricky dynamics in a community mental health team. The coach might respond by saying something like, 'OK, so may I take off my coach hat for a moment and speak as someone who also works in a community mental health team? What I'm thinking may or may not be relevant for you ...'. It is also important for the coach to inform the coachee when the coach hat is going back on. Under most circumstances, it should not be off for long! Claire Pedrick (2020) introduced me to the concept of explicitly changing hats in coaching and I find it particularly useful in my role as an internal coach.[1]

The coach may occasionally offer to contribute a suggestion without being prompted by the coachee. If the coachee declines the offer, then the coach should accept that. Very rarely, it may be relevant for the coach to change hats without specific permission – such as in circumstances where safeguarding, acute mental health or legality issues arise.

We can all slip so easily into giving advice. We do this even when nobody has asked for our advice, even when it is not particularly apposite and even when we ignore it ourselves. I often drink my tea from kitsch mugs with slogans on them. One reads: 'Take my advice, I'm not using it'.

Creating some distance

When deciding on action plans, the coachee can find it helpful to view their situation from a figurative distance. The coach can facilitate this, and it can be done using a variety of perspectives:

- Creating distance using consideration of time, for example, 'Imagine it's a year from now ...' (this is coaching time travel)
- Creating distance using the imagined viewpoint of another person, for example, 'Imagine what X would say ...'

Let us first consider coaching time travel. The coachee can be asked to fast-forward to a year from now and speculate that they have achieved what they wanted and all is going well. The coach can then ask the coachee a range of questions exploring how that outcome came about. Equally, the coach can invite the coachee to fast-forward a year to discover that they did not reach their goal and things are in a right mess. The questions here amount to a pre-mortem, and include enquiry about how that happened. What did they miss that would have prevented that outcome? Box 11.1 offers some questions that employ coaching time travel.

Box 11.1: Coaching time travel

Imagine it is a year from now – things are going well for you – you have achieved your goal of X.

- What did you do to make X happen?
- How did your actions in achieving X fit with your values?
- Who helped you?
- How did they help you?
- What obstacles did you have to overcome?
- What else helped you?
- How did that help you?
- Now you've achieved X, what do you see about your situation and your future?

Of course, the prospection does not need to take the coachee a year hence. It could be, for instance, six months, or five years. The further the coachee imagines into the future, the less specific their answers about what they did to get there are likely to be. The coach can invite the coachee to project forward to their old age (fingers crossed). The coachee is asked to visualize feeling fulfilled at that time, and then asked to imagine what they did to arrive at that point. Their answers tend to reflect the importance of living life according to core values over a prolonged period.

The 'miracle question' was introduced in the 1980s by psychologist Steve de Shazer as part of solution-focused brief therapy practice (de Shazer, 1988). It involves the use of prospection in a particular way that encourages coachees to think deeply about how they might act so as to move forward effectively. A version of the 'miracle question' is shown in Box 11.2.

Box 11.2: A version of the miracle question

Suppose that tonight a miracle happens and your best hopes are achieved. Since you are asleep you will not know that the miracle has happened. When you wake up tomorrow morning, what will be different that will tell you that it has occurred?

The miracle question leads to related questions such as (George et al., 2018):

1 What will be the first sign of the miracle happening?
2 What will you see yourself doing differently that will tell you that the miracle has happened?
3 What will you see others doing differently that will tell you that the miracle has happened?
4 What else do you notice following the miracle?

The miracle question prompts coachees to visualize and consider the nuts and bolts of what they would need to see as clear signs of improvement or progress. The coach can then help the coachee to expand on and extrapolate from what they visualize.

Coaches can also invite coachees to look ahead and give some thought to the nature of their ongoing life beyond attaining their goal. What are the implications of success and the knock-on effects? When planning actions, the coachee should factor in some consideration of how they will cope with their situation if they succeed. We can all think of celebrities who bagged their goals of fame and fortune, and it may well have been better for them if they had not. Conversely, coachees can usefully consider what it might mean for them if they do not achieve their goal. How might they cope and proceed in those circumstances?

In addition to creating distance with coaching time travel as in the examples above, the coach can suggest a shift in perspective by asking the coachee to view the situation through the eyes of another person. What would someone whose judgement the coachee values have to say about the plans they are making?

For some coachees, this envisioned person may be a grandparent (alive or dead), former teacher or a best friend. For others, no-one springs readily to mind. In that case, the question can be adapted and widened. The coach can invite the coachee to consider a role model whom they do not personally know, or even a favourite fictional or historical character (Gilbert and Chakravorty, 2015). The coachee then surmises what that chosen person might advise or do in the coachee's circumstances. Box 11.3 suggests some coaching questions that encourage the coachee to adopt the imagined viewpoint of someone else.

***

Box 11.3: Evoking the coachee's imagined viewpoint of someone else

- What would someone who knows you well and is always on your side (or who knew you well and was always on your side) suggest you should do?
- Is there someone you admire, and whose judgement or approach to life you respect? What do you think they might choose to do in your situation?
- What would a world expert in 'X' say to you?
- What would your favourite fictional character tell you about this?

***

What's the priority?

When the coachee comes to the point of deciding on the actions they will take, the need to prioritize looms large. If you have a daily 'to do' list, I would not be surprised to hear that it contains plenty of items that have been squabbling for your attention for several days (or longer). Some of them will not get done, at least not today. In coaching sessions, as with to do lists, the following question is worthy of consideration. It helps us to focus intentions:

'What's the one thing (you) can do such that by doing it everything else will become easier or unnecessary?' This is the so-called focusing question discussed in the book *The One Thing* (Keller and Papasan, 2013).

It is often not possible for us to narrow down to just one priority task, but it is a worthwhile experiment for us to explore and practise. The focusing question (above) encourages us, in fact, to focus on two aspects. These are first, to prioritize and second, to decide on a relevant course of action.

We can consider a simple example. Imagine you are going for a hike in the Lake District. The reason you are going is to enjoy yourself. On your last walk there, you got soaked and felt frozen to the bone. Being so cold and wet made the trip much less enjoyable. So, staying as warm and dry as possible is a priority for you this time. Your relevant course of action is to buy or borrow an excellent, wet-weather coat. You have identified the relevant priority and the action. Whilst this may seem completely obvious, the truth is that, commonly, we do not prioritize well and the quality of our planning suffers as a result. A coach's questions can help a coachee put first things first and plan more effectively.

A favourite coaching question: What's the most important thing you need to do next?

Of course, prioritizing an action means placing it in the top spot. It also signifies that we need to say 'no' or 'not now' to other tasks and actions. Tim Harford (2015) wrote: 'Every time we say yes to a request, we are also saying no to anything else we might accomplish with the time'.

When we view a request in terms of the opportunity cost, we can see more clearly what is at stake. A coaching question which captures this point has been popularized by coach Michael Bungay Stanier (2016). He asks: 'If you're saying yes to this, what are you saying no to?'

Before I move on from the subject of prioritizing, we should remember the importance of maintaining a sense of balance in our lives as we choose our goals. Coachees sometimes come to coaching conversations to discuss a specific priority in one aspect of their life, for example, in relation to a burning wish for promotion at work. The coachee sets the coaching agenda, but it is legitimate for the coach to ask questions which may highlight the importance of work/non-work balance. There is no doubt that we should seek experiences that nourish us emotionally and physically to avoid becoming depleted. Coachees' action plans need to reflect this fact.

I will add here that those of us working in mental health settings have important and meaningful jobs: to do them well, and for the sakes of ourselves and others, we must also prioritize our own well-being and personal lives. As the saying goes, put your own oxygen mask on first.

There is a strong visual idea which has been attributed to various authors (notably Brian Dyson, 1991) and is relevant here: it is about seeing life as a metaphorical juggling game involving five balls. These balls are work, family, health, friends and integrity. We juggle hard to keep all the balls in the air. Over time, we realize that all the balls are made of glass except the one called work, which is made of rubber. If we drop the work ball, it will bounce, but if we drop the others, then they may be broken forever.

Australian former palliative care nurse Bronnie Ware invites us to carefully consider what we prioritize in our lives. In her book, *The Top Five Regrets of the Dying: A Life Transformed by the Dearly Departing* (2012), she describes the main regrets expressed by the people she looked after. The regrets touch upon:

- being more genuine
- not working so hard
- expressing one's true feelings
- staying in touch with friends
- finding more joy in life[2]

And so? ... Taking responsibility

What will the coachee choose to do and will they actually do it? Building accountability into action plans is important. Usually, the coachee is not accountable as such to the coach, but the coachee is accountable to themselves and to others involved. The question, 'Are you willing to take personal responsibility for doing this?' invites a 'yes' or 'no' response by the coachee and it gets to the point. The coachee comes face-to-face with the reality of doing or not doing what they have said they intend to do. (This is a fundamental question in ThinkOn coaching methodology.)

Reflection on what is at stake can serve to strengthen a person's resolve to execute the action plan. At some time or other, most of us have agreed to do something that we sort of expected we probably would not get around to. 'What's at stake if you don't follow through on your plan?', the coach might ask. We can have a great plan, we can write it down and stick it on the wall, and it will just become rubbish (literally) if we do not act on it.

A favourite coaching question: Are you willing to take personal responsibility to do this?

If the coachee commits to an action plan, the coach should encourage them to decide how they will measure the effectiveness of their plan over time. This requires careful thought. They need to be clear what they are measuring, how and why. This metric can be straightforward, especially in relation to achieving a short-term personal goal that has been discussed in the coaching. For example, a coachee will know within a short space of time whether they did or did not make the important phone call that they said they would make at 9am on the Monday after their last session. Monitoring and evaluating the outcomes of larger scale plans at an organizational level is a much more complicated business.

A point to bear in mind when considering how to measure results is that the process itself can have a distorting effect on the 'thing' being measured. In his book, *The Tyranny of Metrics* (2018), Jerry Muller explains that we cannot use measurement instead of judgement. Measurement is vital, but it needs to be taken in context alongside discernment and experience when reviewing the effect of an action plan. For example, in some mental health services, organizational performance targets set for practitioners focus heavily on the number of service users that practitioners see, with less emphasis on assessing the quality of the care that practitioners provide.

Closing well

As the end of the allotted coaching time draws near, it is useful for the coach to point out how long is left. In the **AR** stages of a coaching conversation, the coach may tend to use more closed questions to good effect, helping the coachee to focus and make choices and plans.

Before a coaching conversation comes to a close, it is important that the coachee has an understanding of their next steps. Usually, by the time the **AR** stages have been completed, the coachee will feel able to name at least one insight that has emerged for them from the conversation, and at least one clear action they intend to undertake. This action is likely to be part of a bigger plan.

Sometimes the important coaching work for the conversation has been done before its scheduled end, and the coach senses that is the case. In such circumstances, it is often sensible for the coaching discussion to close early: the coach simply asks the coachee, 'have we finished?'. In response to this, occasionally coachees might feel they should answer 'yes' even if they do not in fact feel quite finished. The coach needs to consider the tone and delivery of the coachee's answer. If the coachee's 'yes' sounds at all tentative, the coach should check this out and ask if there is anything more they would like to say.

If a conversation continues for the sake of it after the coaching work has been done, this can detract from the overall usefulness of the conversation. To use a baking analogy, we take the carrot cake out of the oven when it is baked, even if the timer has not yet pinged. In the same vein, we finish the coaching conversation when it is done.

At the end of the coaching conversation, coach and coachee need to clarify any arrangements for follow-up contact or further coaching. It is useful for the coach to receive feedback about what the coachee found most useful, which aspects did not work so well and any considerations for next time, if there is to be a next time.

After a coaching conversation has ended, the coachee's internal conversation is likely to continue. It may be useful for them to set aside some buffer time afterwards, so they can carry on thinking for a while before moving on to the next aspect of their day. It is often helpful for coachees to make some brief, summary notes after a coaching conversation, which they can revisit a few days later with any additional insights and reflections. This process increases the likelihood that action steps will be right and relevant.

$$* * *$$

In Part 2 of this book, we have covered practical, wide-ranging coaching guidance. The skills and knowledge presented here are relevant to coaching conversations involving coachees who work in the mental health care field, as well as coachees who are using mental health services. In Part 3, I will focus further on the role of coaching approaches in mental health care with service users and their families, when appropriate and alongside other interventions.

Notes

1   An internal coach is a coach employed within the same organization that employs the coachees.
2   Quoted with permission from Hay House Australia.

References

Bungay Stanier, M. (2016) *The Coaching Habit*. Toronto: Box of Crayons Press.
De Shazer, S. (1988) *Clues: Investigating Solutions in Brief Therapy*. New York: W.W. Norton.

Dyson, B. (1991) Text of Brian Dyson's commencement speech at Georgia Tech, Sept 1991. https://www.markturner.net/2015/05/10/text-of-brian-dysons-commencement-speech-at-georgia-tech-sept-1991/ (accessed 21 July 2021).

George, E., Iveson, C. and Ratner, H. (2018) *BRIEFER: A Solution Focused Practice Manual*. London: BRIEF.

Gilbert, A. and Chakravorty, I. (2015) *Solution Focused Coaching*. Woodhouse Eaves: ThinkOn Books.

Harford, T. (2015) The power of saying no, 20 January. https://timharford.com/2015/01/the-power-of-saying-no/ (accessed 1 May 2021).

Keller, G. and Papasan, J. (2013) *The One Thing: The Surprisingly Simple Truth Behind Extraordinary Results*. London: John Murray.

Muller, J.Z. (2018) *The Tyranny of Metrics*. Princeton, NJ: Princeton University Press.

Pedrick, C. (2020) *Simplifying Coaching: How to Have More Transformational Conversations by Doing Less*. London: Open University Press.

Ware, B. (2012) *The Top Five Regrets of the Dying: A Life Transformed by the Dearly Departing*. London: Hay House.

Part **3**

Coaching Conversations to Improve Clinical Care

Introduction to Part 3

In Part 3, I look in greater detail at the use and value of coaching in the context of clinical care. I argue that when practitioners and clinical managers have coaching skills in their repertoire, they are in a stronger position to work in true collaboration with the people they serve, promoting improvements in the mental and physical health of those people.

In Chapter 12, I explore mental health care and coaching in the context of the recovery approach (Slade, 2013). This approach emphasizes that a person's mental health recovery involves their journey towards achieving important personal goals, and having a sense of purpose, even though their symptoms may not go away completely. This is in contrast to a traditional, 'getting symptom-free' concept of recovery. In addition, Chapter 12 has a focus on coaching in relation to physical health aspects. For a range of reasons, physical health difficulties are linked with increased risk of poor mental health, and vice versa. I take an overview of motivational interviewing, an evidence-based approach often incorporated in health coaching. Motivational interviewing helps people to explore mixed feelings about changing their behaviour in ways that would improve their health, for example, drinking less alcohol.

Chapter 13 outlines a fictional case example, based around clinical experience, where a coaching approach played a part alongside traditional clinical involvement with a man in his early twenties.

In Chapter 14, I show that coaching approaches are a naturally good fit with co-production and co-creation projects. In mental health care terms, the words 'co-production' and 'co-creation' describe the partnership between people who design and provide services and those who use them. I present a fictional case study, again based around clinical experience, to demonstrate the role of coaching in co-creation of a group project.

The final chapter, Chapter 15, is about trauma and offers some suggestions for those who take on coaching roles across a range of contexts. Traumatic events and situations are frequent and diverse. The extent and duration of people's responses to these are complex and varied. Whilst very many people go on to cope and thrive, others are profoundly affected adversely and the effects of trauma manifest in multiple ways.

12 Coaching in clinical care

Introduction

Now is a good time to increase the use of coaching approaches in mental health care. We have entered an age of collaboration and partnership between mental health care practitioners and service users. When mental health care interventions are not set solely by services, but rather decided in mutual agreement with service users, then coaching is a natural fit for this environment.

The coaching skills and knowledge described in earlier chapters are fully relevant for coaching conversations in clinical care when service users are in a position to engage in and make use of such conversations. Adaptation is necessary according to the wishes and circumstances of service users. Practitioners or peer supporters[1] who employ a coaching approach should be aware of limitations and caveats as well as the advantages of coaching.

This chapter examines what we need to consider as we explore the role of coaching in mental health care provision. The chapter is presented in three sections. First, I look at how mental health practitioners have traditionally worked. Historically, they have often placed getting rid of symptoms above other considerations. This focus has, at times, compromised individual service users' personal priorities. I claim that coaching approaches, appropriately used, should be a routine part of clinical support today.

A symptoms focus in mental health care provision is inherently bound up with the idea of 'traditional clinical recovery'. In the second section, I contrast this with the crucial concept of 'personal recovery'. Personal recovery involves a journey to a meaningful life, building resilience and managing mental illness well. Here I draw on the REFOCUS Programme and Intervention (Bird et al., 2014), in which coaching features prominently, demonstrating key REFOCUS values and working practices for mental health practitioners.[2]

Finally, I explore coaching approaches with respect to physical health. Physical and mental health are, of course, not independent entities. They are naturally interconnected with each other and also influenced heavily by related social factors. I claim that practitioners need to have an understanding of the nature of motivation, and how people achieve and sustain behaviour change to benefit their physical health. I elaborate on motivational interviewing.

A natural place for coaching

Clinical mental health work has traditionally involved asking service users problem-focused questions to enable practitioners to gather information, form opinions and offer clinical support. Practitioners trained in medical and traditional health care models may habitually tend to fall into a conversational pattern that boils down to: 'I'll ask you questions and then make some suggestions and recommendations that I hope will be useful'.

This seems a reasonable way to proceed up to a point, but a spirit of genuinely joint endeavour and the addition of coaching style questions can enhance the process and promote the service user's sense of a more hopeful and individually valid direction. As we have seen in earlier chapters, using a coaching style means we listen and ask questions such that the other person moves forward under their own steam in the direction which they have purposely set. In this coaching role, we learn to be quieter and keep out of the way.

The willingness and ability of a service user to engage in a coaching conversation are obviously key factors for practitioners to consider: Does the service user want a coaching style conversation now? Are they in a psychological and cognitive position at the moment to take part fully and benefit? Coaching is a process for facilitating change. So, if a person consistently does not want to change at all, or sees no reason at all to change, then a coaching approach is unlikely to yield much progress. Generally, coaching also involves setting and moving towards goals. If we humans are experiencing extreme emotional distress, disabling trauma or other significant mental disturbance, we are not going to be able to think clearly about future goals and plans at that time.

In such circumstances, practitioners should usually place the greatest emphasis on the practical aspects of care, compassion and often some suitable guidance. In my clinical work, a coaching approach tends to be my default position, but used flexibly to a greater or lesser extent depending on the context. Mental health practitioners must also operate within the scope of their professional codes of conduct and ethical boundaries. The need to respond appropriately to safeguarding, medical or risk issues may mean that the practitioner chooses to adopt a more directive, advisory approach rather than a coach-like one at that time.

When a person has severe cognitive impairment or is otherwise unable to engage with coaching themselves, their family members or carers may find a coaching style of conversation useful. In these situations, if appropriate, practitioners in the care team can offer such conversations to the wider family or carer circle.

At an early stage in someone's recovery journey, a coaching approach might not be what they want or need. But as time goes on, they are often likely to become more willing and able to make use of such conversations.

The coachee/coach positive partnership inherent to a coaching approach not only contributes to some valuable outcomes for service users but, I think also, is likely to have a link with lowered stress for practitioners in the long run. This is because practitioners who habitually use a coaching style are acknowledging that people are responsible for how they live their own lives (with some caveats referred to earlier for people experiencing incapacitating, severe mental illness or impairment).

The role of mental health practitioner is a rewarding one, and at times it can also be depleting. I am sure that all practitioners have experienced interactions in our work when our hearts sang and other interactions when our hearts sank. I have found that a greater number of practitioners than we might suppose gravitate to a semi-conscious, unhelpful assumption of, 'It's completely my job to get this person better', even if they do not use exactly those words to themselves or to others. As we have seen in Chapter 2, the use of coaching can help to dispel that idea and can ease a practitioner's inappropriate sense of excessive responsibility.

Peer supporters are often in a particularly good position to engage in coaching style conversations with service users and carers. Peer supporters can be authentic role models and their stories of lived experience and recovery are sometimes incredibly powerful, showing light at the end of the tunnel, radiating hope.

Coaching and recovery

In mental health terms, the word 'recovery' can mean different things to different people. The traditional understanding of recovery in the mental health field puts emphasis on clinical recovery from illness and reduction or riddance of symptoms – in short, 'getting better'.

However, people can experience personal recovery without necessarily recovering in the traditional clinical sense. Personal recovery means living well and leading a life that is satisfying, worthwhile and enjoyable whilst sometimes still experiencing some symptoms for part, or even most, of the time. A person's recovery journey is unique. The individual concerned is the expert on their personal recovery.

As this journey unfolds, the service user and practitioner collaborate (co-labour): they work together as partners. CHIME is an acronym for five interrelated processes that are key to the personal recovery concept (Leamy et al., 2011).

Box 12.1: The CHIME framework: processes key to the personal recovery concept

Connectedness: having good relationships, support and a sense of community

Hope and optimism: having hope and optimism that recovery is possible; having aspirations and motivation to change

Identity: having a positive sense of identity

Meaning: living a personally meaningful and purposeful life

Empowerment: having a sense of control and agency, awareness of personal strengths, and taking personal responsibility

The extent to which the different CHIME processes each play a part in personal recovery is, of course, different for each person and may change over time. For example, one person may emphasize the importance of reducing symptoms, another may prioritize reconnecting with family, and for someone else spirituality is of key importance..

Whilst the CHIME framework presents an optimistic view of recovery, we must also acknowledge that living with and recovering from mental suffering involves fundamental and sometimes major challenges across multiple aspects of life.

The REFOCUS Programme (2009–2014) was a five-year programme of research funded by the National Institute of Health Research, which aimed to support mental health services to become more recovery-focused (Bird et al., 2014). The REFOCUS Programme led to the development of the REFOCUS intervention.

The purpose of the REFOCUS intervention is to promote effective service user/staff partnerships and to help practitioners develop recovery working practices. Three key mental health service staff values have been identified as particularly supporting recovery and these are shown in Box 12.2 (Bird et al., 2014).

Box 12.2: Three key mental health service staff values supporting recovery

1 The primary goal of mental health services is to support personal recovery
2 Actions by mental health practitioners will primarily focus on identifying, elaborating and supporting work towards the person's goals
3 Mental health services work as if people are responsible for their own lives

---

The three values outlined in Box 12.2 underpin three key recovery working practices that mental health care practitioners need to work towards and uphold if they are to authentically be in recovery-focused partnership with service users (Box 12.3). These partnership relationships are centrally important (Bird et al. 2014).

Box 12.3: Three key mental health service staff working practices supporting recovery

1 Understanding service user values and treatment preferences
2 Working together with service users to assess and amplify their strengths
3 Working together with service users to support their goal striving

---

It is plain to see that coaching plays a prominent role in the development of recovery-promoting relationships and in implementing the working practices shown in Box 12.3. For people embarking on their recovery journeys, encouragement is drawn from a sense that there are people who will not give up on them, and who have faith in them as a person and their resourcefulness. Crucially, practitioners and peer supporters using a coaching style can demonstrate that they retain this faith and confidence.

Below is a list of coaching questions that support the three fundamental recovery working practices of mental health practitioners. To recap, these working practices are:

- Understanding service user values and treatment preferences
- Assessing and amplifying strengths
- Supporting goal striving[3]

Examples of questions that practitioners can ask, aimed at understanding service user values and treatment preferences:

- What matters most to you in life?
- What's the most important thing for people to understand about you?
- What things have the biggest effect on your well-being?
- What have your mental health experiences taught you?
- What do you think is most likely to help you live your life well?
- What has helped before?
- What things could get in the way of you living your life well ... what can you do about them?
- Who do you care about most?

Examples of questions that practitioners can ask, aimed at assessing and amplifying service user strengths to contribute to recovery:

- What is it about you that has helped you get through tough times before?
- What have been some of your best decisions in life?
- What have you felt most proud of?
- What are your most important skills/qualities?
- Who has helped you before and what is it about you that made them want to help?
- How did you help yourself most?
- How have you stopped things getting worse?
- How have you made a positive difference to someone or something?

Examples of questions that practitioners can ask, aimed at supporting service user goal striving:

- What do you most want to happen?
- You mentioned some of your strengths: are there any of those that you'd like to build on especially?
- What would improve your life?
- If you were going to try something new, what would it be?
- What could you do that would make you feel proud?
- When you feel less (for example) depressed, what will you be doing differently?
- What might you like to do that would benefit someone or something?
- What difference might you want to make in the world?

The process of striving to reach goals can be a rich one associated with greater hope, an increased sense of agency and resilience. Of course, the goals should be realistic and specifically relevant, in keeping with the person's values. I again emphasize that practitioners need to acknowledge properly the inherent and frequently wide-ranging challenges associated with mental distress and illness as they support service users' goal striving.

A service user's written action plan might take the form of that in Box 12.4.

Box 12.4: Example of possible components in an action plan

What is my goal?
How will I know I've achieved it?
When do I want to achieve it by?
What's my strongest reason for wanting to achieve this?
How will I do this?
What personal strengths do I have that will help me with this?
Who will help me?
How will I encourage myself?
What might get in the way or hold me back?
How will I reduce the chance of things getting in the way?
What will I do when I have achieved this goal?
What will I do if I haven't stuck to my deadline? (And how much will that matter?)

At a time when demand for mental health care seems particularly great, mental health practitioners, of course, need to consider the practicalities and time implications of how we go about our work. Some practitioners, when they first start to use a coaching approach, fear that this way of working will leave them with insufficient time to cover all the areas of inquiry involved in a thorough assessment or review appointment. With practice, however, mental health practitioners can undertake assessment and implement interventions efficiently in partnership with service users using a valuable coaching stance throughout the whole process.

Let's consider this stance further in the context of mental health assessment. For psychiatrists and other mental health practitioners, clinical terms such as 'presenting problems' and 'history of presenting problems' are likely to be common-place. But in addition to asking 'What's the problem?', it is valuable for mental health practitioners to inquire specifically about a person's preferred future:

- In what way do you want to feel different?
- What would you like to be doing differently?

Questions about family history do not need to focus only on 'Is there any history of mental illness in the family?' Instead, the practitioner using a coaching style might also ask:

- Have any of your relatives been particularly impressive people from your point of view, and in what way were they impressive?

I am not implying that problems and difficult areas should be avoided. As psychologist Steve de Shazer put it, 'We may be solution focused, but we're not problem phobic' (quoted in George et al., 2018).

During mental health assessment and ongoing care, service users need the opportunity to feel heard and validated when they talk about their problems. However, it is clear that a balanced approach is required by practitioners, and if a person who is coming for support continually repeats and emphasizes the negative, they can be creating a pattern of problem reinforcement for themselves. Sometimes the practitioner will need to carefully guide a conversation that has become too convoluted or veered off course. Without taking over, the practitioner can assist the person to return their attention to their agreed priorities.

According to psychotherapist Bill O'Hanlon, practitioners should 'Have one foot in acknowledgement and one foot in possibility' (quoted in George et al., 2018). This means practitioners acknowledge the difficulty that is being expressed and, if appropriate, link it to a possibility question, such as:

- 'I can hear that's been really hard – it sounds like that's something you want to be different in future?'

So, the message in this section is that coaching approaches are key to partnership between mental health service users and practitioners. Coaching is foundational to care that is centred truly on service users' own values, strengths, goals and aspirations.

Coaching and physical health aspects

Let's begin by reviewing why I am writing about physical health in a book about coaching in mental health settings. In population terms (rather than individual ones), those suffering with significant mental ill health are likely to face additional physical health challenges. And those suffering with significant physical ill health are likely to face additional mental health challenges.[4]

People with long-standing mental health difficulties as a group are at an increased risk of impaired physical health, for example cardiovascular disease. Also, these people, in general terms, are likely to live less healthy lifestyles. This is true across a range of psychological or psychiatric problems.

In addition, those coping with chronic physical conditions often face significant related emotional stresses that accompany the pain or restrictions that their illness imposes, for example in severe autoimmune conditions. Many medical conditions, such as Parkinson's disease, inherently involve both physical and mental manifestations of illness.

Social factors, of course, are correlated strongly with people's lifestyles and with their freedoms to choose healthy lifestyles. Severe mental illness has an association with higher rates of poverty (Elliott, 2016), unemployment, less good housing and social isolation, factors that are also linked to poorer physical health.

The reduced energy levels, distraction and lower motivation that go hand in hand with many mental health problems can make it harder for people experiencing such difficulties to choose healthy ways of living. In addition, they may be coping with the side effects of medication, which may include major weight gain and drowsiness.

People may turn to alcohol and cigarettes, or misuse other substances out of habit and in a misplaced effort to feel better. A vicious circle can be established: apathy or hopelessness about the possibility of positive change can take root, and both physical and psychological health deteriorate further.

It is useful to think more about the subject of lifestyle choices. Most of us are knowledgeable about the things we should do to live in a healthy way: for example, reject smoking, eat the right foods in sensible quantities and take exercise. And we all know that being well informed about what to do, on its own, can bear little relation to whether we actually do it, or do it consistently. (And that's the case even when social and financial factors are in our favour.)

Suggestion for you

Think of a time when you decided to make a long-term healthy change to your lifestyle. Be completely honest with yourself as you reflect on this.

- What happened?
- If it worked, what made it successful?
- If it did not work, what would have made a difference to the outcome?

The ways in which people achieve their healthy lifestyle ambitions are not effectively facilitated by health practitioners getting on their high horses, preaching or criticizing. In fact, that approach is likely to have the opposite effect.

And here is where coaching comes in. It represents a more relevant and respectful way to help people move forward. There is potential to improve the outlook for healthy lifestyles when people can develop personally meaningful, realistic lifestyle goals, maintain motivation to reach those goals and sustain their achievements. Through a coaching approach, individuals can gain greater confidence in managing their health and establish some virtuous circles. That is certainly not to imply that these issues are easy or quick to address success-fully. It is worthwhile to accept that lifestyle changes generally involve an element of 'three steps forward, one step back'. That still means two steps forward … and so on.

Motivational interviewing

Motivational interviewing (MI) is a way of communicating with forward focus, in keeping with the essence of coaching and with a track record of aiding suc-cessful behaviour change for healthier lifestyles. An atmosphere of compas-sion and dignity is key.

Motivational interviewing was initially developed in large part by clinical psychologists William R. Miller and Stephen Rollnick.[5] Leaders in the field of motivational interviewing underline that it is an evolving approach rather than a set one, and one where its spirit is more important than the application of particular techniques or tools. In contrast to most coaching approaches, MI and MI style coaching involve a greater degree of guidance by practitioners. Prac-titioners can be straightforward in expressing their views about the potential benefits of change (such as reducing alcohol intake), whilst emphasizing that a person's choices are their own, and the person's actions depend on how willing, able and ready they feel.

There are some key qualities which describe the spirit of motivational inter-viewing. As mentioned, it involves some guidance, but the practitioner is not telling or selling, scolding or moulding. This approach is not about manipulat-ing people to change. Motivational interviewing aims to empower people to make shifts, helping them see their own reasons for change, and their own potential to do it.

For example, motivational interviewing may be helpful for Bella, who suf-fers from anxiety and who has developed a habit of drinking too much alcohol. Bella has mixed feelings about this. On the one hand, she tells herself, 'Red wine helps me cope with stress and lets me un-wind', but on the other hand, she says, 'I know it's not good for me, I'm heavier than I've ever been and I'm often a bit hung over and feel yuk'.

So she feels conflicted about reducing/stopping her drinking, and is not com-pletely sure she wants to make a change. Motivational interviewing can help her to see the advantages of changing her behaviour in relation to alcohol, and to fully appreciate the problems associated with things remaining the same. Having gained clarity about her intention to change, she may be bombarded with self-doubt about her ability to change. MI conversations can help her strengthen her confidence about this ability.

Practitioners and coaches using motivational interviewing need to be proficient in paying attention to the language of change. This involves the practitioner noticing what the person says in terms of the pros and cons about change. When appropriate, the practitioner should endeavour to emphasize the pro-change aspects of the discussion. In motivational interviewing, this is referred to as 'change talk ', in contrast to 'sustain talk', which involves a focus on the situation remaining the same. Practitioners should also keep mindful that both they and the person have relevant expertise and valid opinions about the issues discussed. Information is exchanged in both directions.

The core skills of motivational interviewing are known as the OARS, and as you can see in Box 12.5, they share much in common with core coaching principles.

Box 12.5: The core skills of motivational interviewing

O = asking **Open questions** to allow exploration about what is personally relevant for the person, and to help them see how there is potential and reason for change

A = providing **Affirmation** to give reinforcement for a person's awareness of their own qualities and achievements, so helping to foster their self-belief that they can change

R = promoting **Reflection**, which can include repetition and rephrasing, after attentive and empathic listening by the practitioner

S = **Summarizing** to ensure a mutual understanding of the main themes for the person

---

There are so many conversations taking place every day between service users and practitioners, and these can be seen as chances, even if small and incidental, to address lifestyle challenges that people face and potential lifestyle changes that may be on their minds.

In this chapter, I have explored the place for coaching in clinical settings. In the next chapter, I use a case example to show how coaching principles featured in support of a young man's personal recovery journey.

Notes

1   A peer supporter is a person who uses their own lived experience to support someone else.

2 For further information, see: https://www.researchintorecovery.com/research/refocus/.

3 Goal striving means making a committed effort to attain a goal, developing and maintaining hope and resilience even in the face of setbacks (Bird et al., 2014).

4 https://www.kingsfund.org.uk/projects/time-think-differently/trends-disease-and-disability-mental-physical-health (accessed 31 July 2021).

5 Motivational Interviewing Network of Trainers (MINT). https://motivationalinterviewing.org (accessed 10 July 2021). See also https://psychwire.com/motivational-interviewing/resources.

References

Bird, V., Leamy, M., Le Boutillier, C. et al. (2014) *REFOCUS: Promoting Recovery in Mental Health Services*, 2nd edition. London: Rethink Mental Illness. https://www.researchintorecovery.com/files/REFOCUS%20Manual%202nd%20edition.pdf.

Elliott, I. (2016) *Poverty and Mental Health: A review to inform the Joseph Rowntree Foundation's anti-poverty strategy*. London: Mental Health Foundation. https://www.mentalhealth.org.uk/sites/default/files/Poverty%20and%20Mental%20Health.pdf.

George, E., Iveson, C. and Ratner, H. (2018) *BRIEFER: A Solution Focused Practice Manual*. London: BRIEF.

Leamy, M., Bird, V., Le Boutillier, C. et al. (2011) Conceptual framework for personal recovery in mental health: systematic review and narrative synthesis, *British Journal of Psychiatry*, 199 (6): 445–52. https://doi.org/10.1192/bjp.bp.110.083733.

Slade, M. (2013) *100 Ways to Support Recovery: A Guide for Mental Health Professionals*, 2nd edition. London: Rethink Mental Illness. https://www.rethink.org/advice-and-information/living-with-mental-illness/treatment-and-support/100-ways-to-support-recovery/.

13 A quiet and useful coaching stance in mental health care: a case example

This brief chapter tells part of Isaac's story. It demonstrates the value for a service user of a mental health practitioner's coaching mindset, and of a collaborative, coaching style relationship between these two people. I am not claiming the practitioner's approach was extraordinary or revolutionary: it did not need to be.

Isaac's situation

Isaac was a young man in his early twenties who worked in a bar in a city in Northern England. He had recently split with his girlfriend and Isaac felt that his life was stalling. He was aware of feeling unsettled and was experiencing a rising sense of background worry.

Isaac's occasional use of cannabis started to increase. He began to develop ideas that people at work were plotting to have him sacked, and at night he heard someone trying to get into his flat (or rather, he believed he did). At times, he thought there were 'rats with the power of speech' in the back yard of the bar, there to spy on him. He became erratic at work and sometimes did not show up for his shifts.

After Isaac started a fight at the bar one night, he was picked up by the police, and a mental health assessment followed. Isaac was admitted to a psychiatric ward. He remained there for some weeks, during which time he came to understand part of his recent experience in terms of a psychotic episode – as a loss of being in touch with reality. Isaac's psychotic symptoms subsided. During this period in hospital, gradually, Isaac accepted the medication that he was offered and he had no further cannabis. Isaac talked with the nurses on the ward, and also met with his psychiatrist (he did not meet with a clinical psychologist due to staff shortage in the department).

Before his discharge from the ward, Isaac and his care team talked at length about arrangements for his ongoing support once he returned home. They agreed that he would have 'one-to-ones' with a community mental health team support worker, Bob, plus review meetings with a psychiatrist. Isaac said he would continue to take medication (in the form of tablets) and avoid cannabis. He was allocated a social worker to provide additional support.

After Isaac left hospital, he and Bob met as planned. Their conversations proved valuable for Isaac. The discussions, in part, involved reflection about his progress in relation to symptoms, medication and cannabis. During the weeks after discharge from hospital, Isaac's psychotic symptoms did not return, although he experienced some anxiety and intermittently lower mood. He continued to take his prescribed medication and remained off cannabis. But our focus of interest in the context of this book is Bob's use of a coaching approach in conversation with Isaac, and how this helped Isaac to explore and start to do the following:

- clarify what was important to him in life following his recent experience
- see and appreciate his strengths
- make some plans in line with what was important to him, and playing to his strengths

Coaching style conversations and more

In his conversations with Bob, Isaac concluded he wanted to rebuild significant family relationships that had soured, and he said he needed to make some lifestyle changes. There were important practicalities that Isaac realized he should address (with the assistance of relevant agencies) in relation to his accommodation, finances and future employment.

Isaac also acknowledged to Bob and to himself that, for years, anxiety had been a bigger part of his life than he had previously allowed himself to realize. He was clear that he wanted to follow a different track to the one that had led him to hospital.

Bob listened a great deal and he did so very attentively. He also asked timely questions. Box 13.1 contains examples of questions that Bob asked Isaac as take-off points for his thinking over the course of their conversations.

Box 13.1: Questions for Isaac

What are you like when you are at your best?
When in your life have you felt especially proud?
When in your life have you felt most content?
When in your life did you feel you'd done something very important?
What do you admire most in other people?
What makes you angry in life?
When you were a child, what were you good at?
When you were a child, what did you enjoy doing?

Isaac had not expected that it would feel so straightforward to confide in and trust Bob. We will look in detail at one aspect that was consequential for Isaac during those conversations. As he spoke with Bob, an idea occurred to Isaac that he thought might seem childish: he mentioned tentatively that he had liked painting when he was a child and had felt quite good at it back then.

Bob said he was no art therapist, but proposed they explore Isaac's thoughts about painting a bit more. Bob invited Isaac to expand on and delve into the idea. Bob based his initial inquiry about this on the ThinkOn Thinking Effectiveness Framework (see Chapter 9). He explained that he would ask Isaac some questions, and they could 'see what comes up for you'.

The Thinking Effectiveness Framework prompts a coachee to consider a subject in terms of the statements and questions they ask themselves when they think of that subject. This framework also cues a coachee's memories associated with the issue, and the things they imagine for the future in respect of it. Having undertaken this exploratory process, a coachee may gain a clearer sense of what they want, how they might go about getting it and what might hold them back or get in the way. So, Bob asked the following questions:

> **Bob:** When you think about painting …
> … what sort of things do you say to yourself about it? (statements)
> … what questions come to mind about it? (questions)
> … what memories come to mind about it? (memories)
> … what ideas or hopes for the future come to mind about it? (imagined future)

Isaac spoke at length in response to Bob's questions, and after this exploration, Isaac felt positive about their talk. Below are some of the points that emerged from Isaac's initial reflections during that conversation with Bob.

> **Bob:** When you think about painting, what sort of things do you say to yourself about it?
> **Isaac:** Painting again … I might feel like a kid.
> But it might feel good to do after all this time.
> I could paint whatever I want, and paintings don't need to make sense.
> There's a great colour called cerulean blue.
> **Bob:** When you think about painting, what questions come to mind about it?
> **Isaac:** If I did painting, would it just be sh**?
> Would I feel like I used to when I did painting as a kid? – that was a good feeling.
> Would I go somewhere to paint? Might cost? I don't want to do it with other people.
> I wonder what my Nan would say if she was alive? I always did painting at her house.

Bob: When you think about painting, what memories come to mind about it?

Isaac: When I was painting, I could concentrate without trying to. It was, sort of, a happy thing.

I felt dead proud of one picture that got me a prize. It was a dragon.

I remember in Year 7 when Miss Fletcher told me the blue was called cerulean.

Sitting in Nan's kitchen. She always put my pictures on the wall.

Bob: When you think about painting, what ideas or hopes for the future come to mind about it?

Isaac: I'd like to get that concentration, that good feeling I told you about – don't know if that's just when you're a kid.

I want to paint what I feel like. I mean paint what I want to paint, and paint how I feel.

It'd be good to feel proud about it maybe.

This conversation led them to agree to do some painting together at Isaac's flat during their next few meetings. They followed through on this plan and sometimes Isaac talked a lot as they painted. His conversation ranged from discussion of bottled-up feelings to practical problem-solving. At other times, Isaac was immersed silently in his art. Bob did not say much, but asked some short, prompting questions and maintained a focused presence with Isaac throughout.

When they had first talked about painting, Isaac had been clear that he did not want to do it as part of a group activity. Soon, however, Bob concluded it would be useful to encourage Isaac to reflect on his initial view about this. Bob told Isaac that he had heard about painting sessions offered at a local community centre. Bob used a gently challenging coaching style to develop the discussion whilst emphasizing that any choices were, of course, entirely Isaac's. Bob's questions included:

- What are you assuming about painting in a group at the community centre that puts you off?
- What are you avoiding that is holding you back?

He also asked:

- If you did go to group painting sessions, what might be the biggest benefit for you from going?

In response, Isaac talked about some anxiety about being judged by other people there. He said he thought his painting might not be 'good enough' and people might look down on him if they knew he had been mentally ill. He also suspected that the other group members would probably 'get up my nose'. And he didn't want to be told what to paint by 'some teacher', he liked to do what was in his head.

As the conversation progressed, Isaac acknowledged that what was most important for him about painting was actually doing it rather than the picture at the end of it. And, anyway, going to the community centre might help him improve his painting. He wouldn't need to say anything to people there about his mental health, and there might be 'some okay people' at the centre that he would get along with.

A few days after their conversation, Isaac went to visit the community centre that Bob had mentioned. It was run by a charity providing visual arts facilities. He signed up for a course of painting sessions, two hours once a week in a large art room at the community centre in a group of eight people, 'suitable for all'.

Isaac attended all twelve sessions of the course. It was not art therapy, but certainly he found it rewarding in terms of his well-being. At follow-up appointments with his psychiatrist, in addition to discussion about the specifics of symptoms, medication, side effects and so on, Isaac was keen to talk about the important support and encouragement he had received from Bob, and about doing painting.

Bob had helped Isaac to feel less overwhelmed and more hopeful. Isaac said that after conversations with Bob, he (Isaac) could somehow start to see things in a different way. Isaac said he would never have picked up a paintbrush, or even thought about any painting, without Bob 'asking [him] stuff'.

Isaac explained that painting made him feel awake and, when he was painting, he seemed to have a sort of respect for himself. He could put things into his pictures that he could not put into any words that made sense. Isaac said that although some of the things he created were scary to do at times, he felt his head was 'cleaner' afterwards, and 'more laid-back'. He said painting also led him to notice things more around him and to see the colours better (especially outside, and especially when the sky was cerulean blue). He said that, often, he had decided to walk to the community centre and back, rather than get the bus, so he could see more sky.

Isaac, to his slight surprise, had made some good friendships with others at the painting sessions, and he had enjoyed encouraging other people with their creativity. He said he would be continuing to attend the community centre and had arranged a meeting with a careers adviser. He would love to have some kind of job connected to painting and art if he could.

The part of Isaac's story that we have spotlighted here provides a small but significant example of the usefulness of coaching approaches in a broad model of mental health care – it also points to the power of art. Isaac benefitted from the specialist interventions, including medication, and these were combined successfully with a wider life and well-being focus facilitated by coaching.

Box 13.2 shows established correlates of well-being (Foresight Mental Capital and Wellbeing Project, 2008). Bob's coaching approach contributed to Isaac's discovery of ways to improve his well-being alongside a more traditional model of mental health care.

> **13.2: Ways to improve our well-being**
>
> Connecting with people
> Being active
> Taking notice and savouring the moment
> Continuing to learn
> Doing something for other people

In the next chapter, I will explore a potential role for coaching in the co-production and co-creation of mental health services – that is, in the joint development of services by the people who provide them and the people who use them.

Reference

Foresight Mental Capital and Wellbeing Project (2008) *Mental Capital and Wellbeing: Making the most of ourselves in the 21st century. Final project report.* London: Government Office for Science. https://www.gov.uk/government/publications/mental-capital-and-wellbeing-making-the-most-of-ourselves-in-the-21st-century.

14 Coaching, co-creation and co-production

Introduction

True collaboration between service users and service organizations is key to improving mental health care. 'Co-production is an ongoing partnership between people who design, deliver and commission services, people who use the services and people who need them' (NCCMH, 2019: 5).

In this chapter, I offer a case study that demonstrates a role for coaching approaches in co-production and co-creation. I show how coaching input bolstered the development of a co-created carer support group. This input took the form of one-to-one coaching for the group's founder/leader, and subsequently involved coaching activity within the carer group. The case study presented here is fictional, but draws on my experience of working with a carer support group.[1]

The chapter is in two sections. In the first, I outline the background to the Hope Grove Carer Support Group (HOPE) and the inspiration behind it. Against a backdrop of stretched local mental health services, the father of a 10-year-old son with complex mental and physical health difficulties had a strong desire to make a positive difference for families caring for children with such needs.

I then go on to describe the ways in which coaching featured in the development and ongoing activity of HOPE, initially supporting the founder to translate his hopes into reality and subsequently promoting the resourcefulness of group participants. I include useful techniques and questions that proved valuable in this co-creation journey.

Hope Grove Carer Support Group

> *Never doubt that a small group of thoughtful, committed citizens can change the world.*
>
> – Margaret Mead[2]

The background to HOPE

The Hope Grove Carer Support Group (HOPE) is a group for parents and carers who are supporting a child or young person with learning disability and associated mental health challenges. Caring for children and adolescents with such problems can be a tough experience, at times leading carers to feel isolated, overwhelmed and with a sense of not knowing what is round the corner.

Together with the support of a local mental health service, HOPE was set up several years ago by a father, Tim, who cares for his son Sam. Sam lives with learning and physical disability and has experienced periods of significantly low mood and anxiety.

The history is that prior to setting up HOPE, Tim's family's experiences had provided him with jagged, first-hand knowledge about fault-lines in Learning Disability Mental Health Services (LDMHS) provision in his part of the UK in the 2010s. In particular, the communications from professionals to Tim and his family were inconsistent and patchy, Tim often felt alone and passed from pillar to post in trying to seek the best help for Sam. Practitioners did not always follow through on planned actions, sometimes leaving Tim feeling frustrated, anxious and unheard in relation to Sam's mental health care.

So, Tim decided he wanted to set up a parent carer group, and to support him in doing this, he sought a constructive collaboration with the local LDMHS involved with Sam's care. Tim's aim was to offer help and encouragement to parents and carers struggling with a range of stresses related to caring for young people with difficulties like Sam's.

Tim embarked on this project on an unpaid basis. Ideally, he wanted a LDMHS practitioner to join him in running the group, and access to a LDMHS venue in which to hold the groups. Prior to Sam's birth, Tim had worked as a social worker, and therefore he was also able to draw on this professional perspective.

Tim was emphatic from the start that he did not want the group to be what he termed a 'mega-moan'. He came to the table reminding people that it is easy to complain about mental health services, but the task is for all concerned to acknowledge the problems and, together, to find ways forward that work. Tim was very aware of the complexity of group dynamics and the power of emotion in groups. Therefore, he wanted, as he said, to 'make sure this is a force for good from the start'. He knew that well-intentioned but poorly thought-through efforts might backfire badly.

Tim explained that he wanted to be part of co-production not faux-production. He wanted to achieve real partnership with LDMHS, not merely a veneer of it. HOPE was initially run on a voluntary basis and subsequently became a commissioned service.[3] It is an example of what can be done when energy, motivating values and creative thinking come together.

What HOPE became

HOPE groups meet monthly on a drop-in basis at a LDMHS centre, and the groups follow a structure that is broadly the same each time. There are discussions about topics chosen by the group, and time for informal conversation, including sharing experiences and practical tips. Guest speakers are sometimes invited to talk and answer carers' questions. An experienced and approachable

LDMHS nurse, Tammy, joins the groups. Within this structure, there is flexibility to ensure the process is relevant to the needs of those there on the day.

There is a HOPE e-network and a range of opportunities for carers and parents to take part in consultation work about the ongoing development of LDMHS. In addition, HOPE coordinates some community events and activities for families. In recent years, families, service users and professionals have provided a great deal of positive feedback about HOPE.

During Covid-19 pandemic restrictions, HOPE had to adapt and was needed more than ever. Groups met only virtually for many months, and of course this added a different dimension to the group process.

Tim had the original vision and vitality to breathe life into the HOPE project. I will show how Tim's conversations with Sarah (both a mental health practitioner and professional coach) were useful in establishing HOPE and maintaining its progress. HOPE has faced barriers and bumps along the way. It has not always been easy for Tim and Tammy (LDMHS nurse) to maintain clear vision and stamina in the face of these. Tim's coaching conversations with Sarah have helped.

Tim has gone on to develop his own coaching skills and he now takes the role of coach in conversations with the LDMHS manager three times a year.

Coaching and the Hope Grove Carer Support Group

Coaching played an important role in the development and progress of HOPE in the following ways:

- One-to-one coaching conversations for Tim (with Sarah, a coach who is also an experienced mental health practitioner)
- Coaching style activities within the HOPE groups themselves, facilitated initially by Sarah and subsequently by Tim.

Let's consider each of these in turn.

One-to-one coaching

At the time of Tim's initial ideas about setting up a parent carer group, he approached Sarah to join him in thinking about the development of HOPE. He knew of her from his contact with LDMHS, and she was able to become involved. Tim and Sarah met for one-to-one coaching conversations on a number of occasions during the early months of the HOPE project. Subsequently, the two had some further coaching conversations at Tim's request. The discussions followed the CLEAR framework incorporating elements of the ThinkOn® solution-focused approach (Gilbert and Chakravorty, 2015; see Chapter 5).

These sessions helped Tim to prioritize his many ideas, and channel his energy into clear goals and action steps. His authentic intention to achieve positive change was clear from the outset. Tim's confidence to tap into and believe in his own creativity fluctuated. However, his self-belief about achieving his aims consolidated as his hard work started to reap results. Coaching conversations provided an opportunity for Tim to reflect and build further on this confidence.

Extracts from one-to-one coaching conversations

The following part of this section contains a collection of extracts from coaching conversations between Tim and Sarah about the HOPE group at its inception. At that point, Tim had gained general, but not specific, agreement from mental health service managers for co-production with the local LDMHS.

The focus here is on the coaching questions and on Tim's answers. For clarity, the conversational padding has been omitted in the extracts below.

Sarah: What do you want to achieve?

Tim: A group meeting every month for parents and carers, so they can give and get support, get help and guidance – with a mental health professional there too, so it's families working together with professionals ... (I'm making notes here 'cos I want to have this neat in my head.)

Sarah: What do you want to achieve first?

Tim: Gotta make sure LDMHS at Hope Grove is really on board for a regular carer group, I want LDMHS to know this is needed – that this will be good news for families and good news for LDMHS, that carers should be listened to and we have something to offer. We'll get people coming to a group ... need to let carers know about the group ... just have to go for it. I need a LDMHS worker like Tammy, and a room at the Hope Grove Centre. But, yes, really the first thing is to talk again to the LDMHS manager about the ins and outs and practical things.

Sarah: How much do you want to achieve this: setting up the carer support group together with LDMHS (score out of 10, with 10 being you really want to achieve it)?

Tim: I'm really clear I want to achieve it, 10 out of 10. Fifteen out of 10!

Sarah: What is your strongest reason for wanting to do it?

Tim: My family has been through a lot, and it's been tough. I really want to make things better for other people in that situation. I want people to know they're not on their own and they can do things that will help. And they'll get heard. And I want LDMHS people to make sure they really think about parents and carers too.

Sarah: How achievable do you think it will be to get the carer group up and running together with LDMHS (score out of 10, with 10 being definitely achievable)?

Tim: Hand on heart, I can't say what exact score ... but we are going to do it. So I'll say 9½.

Sarah: How will you know when you've successfully achieved what you set out to do?

Tim: Parents and carers will be coming to groups, they'll feel they can say what's on their minds and they'll know they are being listened to, they'll say they have some hope back. They'll feel there's practical stuff they can do to improve things. That's how I'll know.

Sarah: What are your particular strengths in this situation Tim?

Tim: I'm a determined person – my old teacher at school used to call me Tenacious Tim. I can think outside the box. I work hard, I pay attention to things that I know matter. The thing is, I'm genuine and I care about families. It's good that I've had experience in social work, so I know a bit about how people tick. I'm a last-minute person, but I always get things done somehow when it's important.

Sarah: What's the key thing to do to achieve this?

Tim: We've got to get people with us: we'll get carers coming along, and we'll have support in the groups from the right professionals. We need solid LDMHS involvement for it to work, and we've got to make sure the group is totally about what families need.

Sarah: How will you get the right people in LDMHS to help?

Tim: I'll talk to anyone I need to in LDMHS, and to be honest, how on earth can they turn their backs on it. And we just want to start small. I want to get this going with support from professionals 'cos things get complicated. We've got to be together on it.

Sarah: What could hold you back?

Tim: Disapproval from people working in the service – high-ups or people with a big say who could stick a spanner in it if they wanted. One professional I spoke to about it was so negative and I felt like I'd been told I was just a difficult person with a crap idea. But actually you know, thinking about it: f*** it, that's made me more determined. But we will have to pay attention to the practical things.

Sarah: How will you overcome hurdles?

Tim: I'll keep at it – but I know that sometimes you need to think what needs doing different if things aren't working. I'll get people I can trust to help. I wasn't born yesterday and I can face it that I'm not always right (… on the rare occasion I'm wrong!!).

Sarah: How will you keep brave in the face of setbacks?

Tim: Because of what we've gone through as a family I know that I'm brave. I have got courage actually. Just 'cos things are hard or frightening or get you chewed, that doesn't mean you give up. I know that setbacks will happen, but these could be like our best lessons … and people who make things difficult can be like our teachers. But it doesn't feel like it at the time! At the end of the day, I know I want to do this for the right reasons, and I know that most people working in services want to do a good job. The carer group won't be about always moaning on about services, it'll be about doing something to make things better, and doing something that's missing.

Sarah: How will you know if you need to change course?

Tim: I don't know … I guess if nobody comes to the groups, or if things aren't working out at all after a few months. For me, when things don't go right, first I get p'd off, then after a while I see things different, and then I get back up and try to do what needs doing.

Sarah: So, given all you've said ... what will you do?

Tim: I'll talk again to the LDMHS manager – and I'll really properly plan what I want to say before. Get a room sorted, and check about Tammy (that canny nurse) joining us. We want to start and see what happens. We'll start monthly groups at the Centre on a Thursday night, and word will spread and people will come. We'll do it, we'll have to be smart, think on our feet and learn. I've got a head full of ideas about all this.

Sarah: How confident are you that you'll put your plans into action?

Tim: A hundred percent!

Sarah: When will you start to do it?

Tim: Okay – I'll arrange another meeting with the LDMHS people, then when I get the room arranged, we'll set the date and get posters about the group up at the Centre. Yes, today I'll see about the LDMHS meeting. In fact, by lunchtime. I'm going to write out some of these scrappy notes I've made while we've been talking ... I'm a man with a plan.

When Tim looks back to the time that he decided to set up HOPE, he says that he did not know what he did not know, and he is amazed at how much he learnt and achieved. His conversations with Sarah gave him constructive space to reflect, to explore his motivation and his relevant strengths. In connection with this reflection and exploration, he considered practicalities about his goals and decided on his action steps. Box 14.1 provides examples of some questions that helped to stimulate Tim's thinking.

Box 14.1: Examples of Sarah's coaching questions for Tim

What do you want to achieve?
What do you want to achieve first?
How much do you want to achieve this? (score out of 10)
What is your most important reason for wanting to do it?
How achievable do you think it will be? (score out of 10)
How will you know when you've achieved it?
What are your particular strengths in this situation?
What's the key thing to do to achieve this?
How will you get the right people to help?
What could hold you back?
How will you overcome hurdles?
How will you keep brave in the face of setbacks?
How will you know if you need to change course?
So, given all you've said ... what will you do?
How confident are you that you'll put your plans into action?
When will you do it?

Coaching style activities within HOPE group meetings

Once HOPE group meetings had become more established, Tim's spirit of initiative went from strength to strength. He was keen to explore with Sarah how coaching type activities could also be used during group meetings to connect participants with their own resourcefulness and sense of agency.

Initially, Sarah joined the group meetings informally on a few occasions to facilitate coaching activities. Tim and Tammy (his LDMHS nurse colleague in the group) quickly became familiar with some of the coaching principles and Sarah withdrew from the coaching facilitator role.

A coaching style activity that proved popular and valuable in HOPE meetings used a technique from ThinkOn® (Gilbert and Chakravorty, 2015), the 20 Answers technique. I outline this below. You may say, 'Well, that's brainstorming and making a list', and you would not be wrong. However, the technique amounts to more than a bit of brainstorming and list writing because it involves a systematic process that leads to some specific prioritizing and planning.

The ThinkOn 20 Answers technique: moving from a problem to a solution

Here are the steps for participants to follow:

- Write down the problem in a sentence.
- Turn the problem statement into a constructive/helpful question rich with possibility, starting with:
  - What could I possibly ...? OR
  - How could I possibly ...? OR
  - Who could possibly ...?
- Then begin to generate ideas to move from a problem to a solution, and write them down in a numbered list. This could be done as a group activity from the outset, with people chipping in ideas while someone writes on a flip chart. However, the exercise is more powerful if people spend some time generating their own individual list (Furnham, 2020) before they join together to come up with a collective group list. (The coach/facilitator can give it the feel of a game, setting a timer to ping when the time is up for the individual lists, for example, after five minutes.)
- Ask people to aim to generate at least 20 ideas in a short space of time – not thinking the ideas through in detail, but just generating suggestions as possibilities.
- Once the list has been completed, read back through it and highlight or asterisk the numbers for the five best ideas – that is, those that would contribute most to solving the problem.
- Of those, which is the top one? How, when and with whom will you start putting it into action?

When people set to work generating their own 20 possible answers, it is quite usual for them to find that they get stuck after a few obvious ideas. A suggestion from the coach at that point is for them to let their minds roam free and to entertain ideas that may seem completely ridiculous. An interesting observation is that if people allow their thoughts to foray into imaginative territory, when they haul themselves back to reality they may have a new perspective. Their pie in the sky diversion may have produced a valuable realization about possibility.

A further point to make about this 20 Answers exercise is that whilst you might expect the top five asterisked ideas to be the five that were generated first, this is far from always the case.

Tim talks about a coaching session where idea number 12 on his possible answers list emerged as an important way forward. Idea number 12 had previously not entered his thoughts at all. This emphasizes the potential value in squeezing our brains for options. The note of caution is that we should then properly consider and prioritize them, to then focus down to action steps: a random pile of unprocessed option ideas can lead us to feel confused. But if an unforeseen lightbulb moment at, say, idea number 16 is honed into a plan, the exercise has contributed to clarity and forward movement.

Part of what accounts for the success of the 20 Answers technique is that it helps those involved realize they have more power in situations than they may have otherwise assumed. The experience of being encouraged to think broadly can feel like stepping out of a crowded, cramped space into a wide, open area where it seems possible to move more freely, breathe more deeply and see fresh perspectives. It can also feel like fun.

Here is a case example of HOPE using the ThinkOn 20 Answers technique as a way of generating ideas, discussion and action points. It began when Nadine, a carer, spoke about a problem she was facing:

- 'I don't have enough time or opportunity to look after myself'.

This was a statement that most of the group could identify with, and Tim suggested they use the 20 Answers technique to think about it. He said he would talk the group through the technique and would take part in the activity himself. People were free to opt out, but all fourteen chose to participate. Tim made sure they all had pen and paper, and he began by explaining they would look at the problem statement and flip it into a question. So, the problem statement, 'I don't have enough time or opportunity to look after myself', was turned into a question:

- 'How could I possibly free up more time or opportunity to look after myself?'

Tim asked everyone to work quietly for five minutes on their own, generating possible answers. He set a timer and joined in by writing his own list. As the minutes ticked by, he gave some brief encouragements, emphasizing nothing was too small or silly to be included in people's lists.

When the time was up, Tim invited group members to choose some of their ideas to discuss with the group. He gave a brief reminder to people to feel free to speak, and some lively discussion followed over the next 45 minutes. This was an important subject, but the atmosphere was not grave and there was a sense of all working together.

Listed below are some of the ideas and intentions that group members generated for increasing time and opportunity to look after themselves.

1 Keep reminding myself not to feel guilty about wanting a bit of time just for me – I'm best at looking after her when I've looked after me.

2 Leave the jobs that don't need doing, and let go of fussing about them.

3 Sleep when I get the chance. (Sometimes I could take a quick nap in the day, and I end up not bothering. But I get so tired 'cos I'm up in the night with Leo – he's having more fits at night.)

4 Accept offers of help from other people.

5 Join in with the kids playing … the other day it was hot – they were splashing in the paddling pool. I got in there with them and we all had a proper good time, don't care that I looked like a beached whale. It was a different way of looking after myself.

6 Put on some lipstick.

7 Do tasks with friends when I can – feels less like work.

8 Notice the good things about everyday stuff. When I wash up, I like watching what happens with the soap bubbles.

9 Cook or bake like I'm pretending to be on telly – I might as well be creative.

10 While the kettle is coming to the boil, I look at things out the window. I often watch a robin. It's me-time. Same when I'm waiting for toast to pop up.

11 Buy myself some yellow flowers.

12 Be more cheerful about having to walk the dog, rather than grumpy – remember, she's a friend, and walking is good for my health.

13 I need to get better at saying 'no' when I've already got too much to do.

14 Every night, I could write down one thing to be glad about from the day.

15 Plan and organize things better when it's possible.

16 Get a colouring book to colour during quiet moments.

17 When I have to wait while Shelley is in appointments, I relax and read the magazines and get a cuppa from the machine. And I don't need to feel bad about it. (They should always get good magazines for waiting rooms!)

18 Stop my habit of blaming myself and make a point of noticing what I'm proud of.

19 Look for the good in people – it makes you feel better than noticing the worst in them.

20 Come to HOPE!

At the end of the activity, Tim asked everyone to make a note of their own personal top three ideas, the ones that they would act on and when. He said that there would be time at the next group for people to feed back about how they got on putting some of the ideas into action.

Coaching principles became embedded into the routine functioning of HOPE: coaching conversations will continue to support the progress and evolution of this and other co-produced and co-created projects.

Suggestion for you – try using the ThinkOn 20 Answers technique (paraphrased with permission)

- Sit down quietly by yourself and think of a problem you are facing
- Write down the problem in a sentence
- Turn the problem statement into a constructive/helpful question that is possibility based, starting with, for example:
  - What could I possibly …? OR
  - How could I possibly …? OR
  - Who could possibly …?
- Answer it 20 times. Be determined to come up with 20 answers
- Read through your 20 ideas
- Which are the best to help address the problem?
- Which will you act on?
- When will you act on them?
- Any surprises about what you have decided?

Notes

1 The Rollercoaster Parent and Carer Support Group is an award-winning project in the North East of England for parents and carers who are supporting a child or young person with an emotional or mental health problem. Rollercoaster was set up by two carers in collaboration with their local community child and adolescent mental health service. The main founder, Wendy Minhinnett, continues to lead the group and is involved in regional and national work related to co-creation and the improvement of mental health services. Website: https://www.rollercoasterfamilysupport.co.uk/. E-mail: support@rollercoasterfs.co.uk.

2 Attributed to Margaret Mead, but the source of this quote appears to be disputed. Please see the Disputed section of https://en.wikiquote.org/wiki/Margaret_Mead.

3 A commissioned service is care or support that is funded and arranged by a public authority such as the National Health Service.

References

Furnham, A. (2020) *Psychology 101: The 101 Ideas, Concepts and Theories that Have Shaped Our World*. London: Bloomsbury.

Gilbert, A. and Chakravorty, I. (2015) *Solution Focused Coaching*. Woodhouse Eaves: ThinkOn Books.

National Collaborating Centre for Mental Health (NCCMH) (2019) Working Well Together: Evidence and tools to enable co-production in mental health commissioning. London: NCCMH. https://www.rcpsych.ac.uk/improving-care/nccmh/other-programmes/coproduction.

15 Coaching and trauma

Introduction

What do we mean by trauma? The word is used to describe a range of harmful or distressing situations which interfere significantly with people's lives and usually pose a substantial threat to physical or psychological well-being. The word trauma is not straightforward to define, and the range of traumatic situations is wide and varied, including events such as a car accident, or the experience of childhood neglect over a number of years. The term trauma is also often used to describe the psychological and physical aftermath of those situations.

This chapter looks at trauma and some implications for coaching: it provides broad rather than very specific information on the subject. I begin by considering the nature and effects of trauma. It is a complex phenomenon which not only can be triggered in multiple ways, but also manifests in multiple ways. Powerful early childhood trauma can have an impact on brain development and can cast a dark shadow into adult life.

I then present elements of coaching practice which are especially relevant in the context of trauma. There are three considerations that I highlight in particular. First, I argue that coaches need to be alert to the possibility that a coachee has been affected by trauma. Secondly, where trauma exists, it is usually helpful for coaches to make the coaching process as predictable as possible. Finally, coaches should also provide clear choice to the coachee, so they can opt out of various coaching techniques or lines of questioning if trauma is being re-triggered.

The many faces of trauma

Trauma occurs if someone undergoes an experience which distresses or harms them to an extent that their usual cognitive, emotional and physiological coping mechanisms are overwhelmed.

We all have some propensity to be traumatized, and the extent to which we are each prone varies considerably depending on a host of interacting, overlapping factors. These include our previous experiences and relationships, our psychological tendencies, our physiology and our genes (Foulkes, 2021). When a person experiences trauma, a trigger event activates their propensity to be traumatized. The combination of trigger and propensity is required if trauma is to follow.

Because as individuals we are variously susceptible to trauma, an event which sparks a pronounced trauma response for one person may not do so for another. Indeed, very many people who experience distressing and disturbing events never develop a lasting or severe trauma response. But people who do have a greater propensity and vulnerability to be traumatized can suffer considerably and over a prolonged period. This is very individual territory. No-one will live a life completely free of traumatic situations, and the range of these situations and the range of human responses to them is vast and variable.

Let's move on to consider an overview of the effects of traumatic experiences. Patterns of emotion, thinking and behaviour can be skewed by trauma in a long-term way, leading to unfulfilled potential as well as suffering. There can be associated problems with relationships, identity and self-regulation, and a wide variety of health issues, as well as more defined post-traumatic stress symptoms.[1]

Box 15.1: Manifestations of trauma

Post-traumatic stress symptoms include:
Horrid intrusive memories and flashbacks
Nightmares
Avoidance of reminders of the trauma
Increased arousal
Feelings of dread
Physical sensations

Other potential mental and physical health difficulties associated with trauma:
Anxiety
Depression
Substance misuse
Personality difficulties
Self-harm
Eating problems
Psychotic experiences
Dissociative experiences (when the mind disengages in situations perceived as threatening)
Chronic physical pain
Impairment in how hunger or tiredness is registered
Interference with memory processes and concentration
Worsening/triggering of some physical health conditions such as asthma, digestive problems, high blood pressure, eczema

---

We should also remember that the experience of significant mental or physical ill health is in itself often traumatic, so there is a compounding effect.

The subject of complex early life trauma merits specific attention in this chapter. The abuse, harm or neglect, especially at the hands of people who are supposed to be caring for a child, can have a highly disruptive effect on development (Ellis and DeJong, 2019). Practitioners and coaches should be aware that such trauma in early childhood can change the way the brain and nervous system develop. There are complex neurobiological and hormonal processes at work.

To aid our understanding of the developmental impact of trauma, it can be useful to think about the difference between a 'learning brain' and a 'survival brain' (Ford, 2009). A *learning brain* is focused on exploration of the environment – this is how the brain gains new information. A *survival brain*, in contrast, is on the lookout for threats – it is poised for rapid, automatic defence with the deployment of stress responses. For children who have experienced serious and sustained threat or trauma, the survival brain tends to operate in overdrive during childhood and beyond. This can compromise the development of the learning brain in the long term.

Having discussed the damaging potential of trauma, I want to give some focus to the concept of post-traumatic growth (Tedeschi and Calhoun, 2004), sometimes known as trauma-related growth. This refers to the experience of positive change that may occur as a result of dealing with highly challenging life circumstances. Following trauma, there can be potential for increased resilience, greater appreciation in life, more meaningful relationships, and clarification of values, priorities and purpose. The idea is that sometimes people not only have the capacity to bounce back from truly awful experiences, they also can bounce forward.

In his book *The Happiness Hypothesis* (2007), psychologist Jonathan Haidt concludes that adversity can have a strengthening effect on people, particularly if they encountered it and overcame it in their twenties. Indeed, they might possibly be happier than if they had not experienced it. Stressful experiences that do not trigger an ongoing avalanche of overwhelm might potentially serve to inoculate a person against the effects of future stress to some degree.

'Kintsugi' apparently means joined with gold in ancient Japanese (de Botton, 2019). Let's consider this in an analogical context of trauma-related growth. Kintsugi is a concept drawn from Japanese philosophy and relates to pottery. The idea of Kintsugi is that pots or bowls that break should not be just thrown away or left out of sight. They should be repaired carefully, with awareness and consideration. Kintsugi involves joining the broken pieces and making the break lines strong and unashamedly coloured with gold, not hidden. This shows respect for what is damaged. It demonstrates that a restored, different and wonderful version can be created from what was once broken. We can apply this concept to people: ourselves and those around us.

Coaching with awareness of trauma

Of course, we should bring our understanding of trauma to our work as coaches and mental health practitioners. A trauma-informed approach (Harris and Fallot, 2001) to health care and coaching offers someone who has experienced trauma an environment where they can feel safe and have trust.

In clinical contexts, we should bear in mind the possibility that trauma features to a greater or lesser extent in the past and/or current reality of many people using mental health services. The coach needs to be able to recognize trauma, should clearly inform the coachee/service user about what to expect about the coaching process, and should let them know that they have choice about how they participate. It is particularly important that roles, boundaries and confidentiality issues are clear to the coachee, promoting trust and emotional safety in the coaching relationship.

Box 15.2 illustrates areas about which the coach needs to be especially mindful in relation to trauma (Vaughan Smith, 2019).

Box 15.2: Good coaching conditions in relation to trauma

The coaching conversation feels safe and 'contained' for the coachee
The coachee knows they have free choice about participating in all aspects of the conversation
The coach explains the coaching process, so the coachee knows what to expect
The coach can recognize trauma, and is mindful of its potential presence
The coach responds consistently calmly, flexibly and with compassion – reducing risk of re-traumatization for the coachee

---

Given that the effects of trauma can involve rapid changes in emotional state, the coach should remain alert for shifts of the coachee's behaviour or emotion that indicate they are not in a position to use their learning brain, and that their survival brain has 'kicked in'. Coaches also need to understand and remember that a variety of sensory perceptions can trigger re-traumatization, sometimes out of the blue. To illustrate this in a non-traumatic context, consider for a moment the power of certain pleasant smells to evoke emotions and memories.

As we know, a degree of constructive challenge from the coach is usually key to coaching style conversations, as elaborated in Chapter 9. A coachee who has suffered trauma, and who is operating predominantly in survival brain mode, will likely be more prone to perceive challenge as threat when the coach intended nothing of the sort. Attuned coaches will factor this in when considering how and when to challenge.

The concept of 'parts of ourselves' can be helpful in coaching those with trauma (Vaughan Smith, 2019). For example, when a coachee thinks about their goals and how to achieve them, it serves them well to consciously and deliberately connect with the resourceful part of themselves. A part of them may think that a particular goal is attainable, while another part of them feels too fearful to attempt it. The coach can acknowledge out-loud if they are hearing and seeing the different parts. The coach can focus inquiry to emphasize the coachee's more confident part, and de-emphasize the self-doubting part, to support the coachee to build a greater sense of empowerment.

Both coachee and coach will work together more effectively when they pay attention in the moment, remaining in what coach and psychotherapist Julia Vaughan Smith calls 'the here and now rather than the there and then'. If it seems appropriate, a coach might invite a coachee to be attentive to the signals from their body and take note of them. The coach might suggest the coachee explores what they feel in their body as they consider an aspect of a goal. Tuning into the body can provide useful guidance, but caution is required.

Some body awareness/mindful awareness practices have the potential to trigger re-traumatization[2] and coaches need to be aware of this. An example of this could be a coach working with a coachee who is thinking about how they will prepare for an important interview. The coach might suggest that the coachee try some mindful breathing during the coaching session, placing close attention on their in and out breath. The coachee starts this, but within a few moments exclaims that they do not like it and want to stop. The coach sees that the coachee is not merely finding the mindful breathing a bit odd, but is becoming distressed. The coachee explains that, although now well, they suffered severe breathing difficulties due to Covid-19 infection some months previously and had been admitted to hospital. The focus on breathing had rekindled some of that experience.

As mentioned in Chapter 10, sometimes words alone are not the best way to stimulate insights and effective thinking. Some coachees may feel more able to explore and express themselves with the incorporation of drawing, use of objects or movements. When there is a history of trauma, non-verbal expression or the use of props may at times feel more suitable or safe for a coachee.

Coaches should take steps to provide a settled context that facilitates the coachee's constructive thinking. When the coach is calm, this can help a coachee attain and maintain their own steadiness. Coaches need to know about their own psychological state going into a coaching conversation. They require personal insight about potential effects of their own life experience of harrowing events. The concept of the 'wounded healer' may be relevant. This refers to the idea that mental health practitioners' career choices are sometimes influenced by an earlier personal history of psychologically wounding experiences.

In the course of their jobs, mental health practitioners are likely to hear distressing tales of trauma and witness upsetting situations on a frequent basis. Hearing painful details of someone's early life abuse, or seeing their tormented loneliness or self-inflicted wounds, has an impact. The steadfast action of being authentically alongside people during the throes and fallout of extreme mental suffering can take its toll. Mental health practitioners can thereby experience traumatic effects second hand (known as secondary trauma).

As described in Chapter 2, supervision can lead coaches to develop greater understanding of what might be going on emotionally for themselves as well as for the coachee. I will re-emphasize that dedicated coaching supervision is required to help coaches to be at their best and give of their best.

> **Suggestion for you**
>
> - Sit quietly for a moment: notice, label and acknowledge your current predominant **emotion(s)**, where possible, not getting tangled in thoughts.
> - Sit quietly for a moment: notice, label and acknowledge your current predominant **physical sensations**, where possible, not getting tangled in thoughts.
>
> Note: Our emotions and sensations can often be named in single words, whereas our thoughts usually take the form of sentences.

This chapter has given us pause for thought about coaching and trauma. Shifting focus, in the fourth and final part of the book our attention will be on coaching for the workforce of mental health care organizations.

Notes

1 https://www.blueknot.org.au/Resources/Information/Understanding-abuse-and-trauma/What-is-complex-trauma/Complex-Trauma-and-mental-health (accessed 10 July 2021).
2 https://davidtreleaven.com/ (accessed 21 July 2021).

References

de Botton, A. (2019) *The School of Life: An Emotional Education*. London: Penguin.

Ellis, J. and DeJong, M. (2019) Complex post-traumatic stress disorder in children and adolescents, *CPD Online*. https://elearning.rcpsych.ac.uk/learningmodules/quickbitecomplexpost-trauma.aspx (accessed 11 July 2021).

Ford, J.D. (2009) Neurobiological and developmental research: clinical implications, in C.A. Courtois and J.D. Ford (eds.) *Treating Complex Traumatic Stress Disorders: An Evidence-Based Guide*. New York: Guilford Press.

Foulkes, L. (2021) *Losing Our Minds: What Mental Illness Really Is – and What It Isn't*. London: Vintage.

Haidt, J. (2007) *The Happiness Hypothesis: Putting Ancient Wisdom to the Test of Modern Science*. New York: Arrow Books.

Harris, M. and Fallot, R.D. (2001) Envisioning a trauma-informed service system: a vital paradigm shift, *New Directions for Mental Health Services*, 2001 (89): 3–22. https://doi.org/10.1002/yd.23320018903.

Tedeschi, R.G. and Calhoun, L.G. (2004) Posttraumatic growth: conceptual foundations and empirical evidence, *Psychological Inquiry*, 15 (1): 1–18. https://doi.org/10.1207/s15327965pli1501_01.

Vaughan Smith, J. (2019) *Coaching and Trauma: Moving Beyond the Survival Self*. London: Open University Press.

Part **4**

Coaching within Mental Health Care Organizations

Introduction to Part 4

So far in this book we have explored the skills, knowledge and attitudes on which great coaching is built. We have also examined how these can be applied to clinical mental health service settings.

In Part 4, we visit the subject of organizational coaching within the workforce. It is reasonable to expect that services will be better when staff responsible for providing them really listen, reflect, and feel both personally and collectively resourceful. Similarly, it is legitimate to hope that staff will be more content, loyal and high-performing in a working environment where listening, constructive reflection and resourcefulness are prized by leaders and colleagues.

Chapter 16 outlines what is meant by a coaching culture, whereby many conversations and management practices within an organization are routinely underpinned by coaching principles. My main focus here is on internal coaching. This is where a trained coach who is also employed in the same organization as the coachee engages in one-to-one formal coaching conversations. To make a case for internal coaching, I demonstrate some of the core elements of an internal coaching initiative for psychiatrists that I developed, with the support of the medical directorate, in a large mental health care organization in Northern England.

Then, in Chapter 17, I argue that we need to weigh up special considerations that come into play when the coach and the coachee are part of the same organization. In addition to my own experience, I draw on the work of Katharine St. John-Brooks (2018), coach and author.[1] Potential ethical dilemmas are prominent, as is the concomitant need for supervision. I use case studies to demonstrate coaching practices.

16 Coaching: the organization and the workforce

Introduction

This chapter is divided into two parts, the first of which presents an overview of 'coaching culture'. It argues that those in charge of mental health care organizations who espouse such a culture should be clear about what they hope to achieve, and how they will review the value of a coaching culture.

The second section explores one important aspect of coaching culture, namely 'internal coaching'. When embedded in a wider coaching culture, I argue that internal coaching initiatives can support the personal and professional development of individual employees. Hand-in-hand with these individual benefits, I strongly suggest there are also associated gains for teams and services.

I then highlight some key procedural aspects of internal coaching work that I undertook with psychiatrists. The aim of the internal coaching initiative was to support the developmental aspect of the appraisal process for psychiatrists. Feedback in relation to this aim was positive and, in addition, we concluded that the initiative had a possible role to play in the retention and well-being of the mental health service workforce.

Coaching culture

What does a coaching culture look like? What do we see when coaching conversations form a fundamental part of how the everyday work is done? A visit to a successful organization with an established and thriving coaching culture will reveal a workforce engaged in values-driven, solution-focused discussions and constructive reflection about the work (Parsloe and Leedham, 2017). Of course, this is not to say that everything in the garden will be consistently rosy.

> **Box 16.1: What would you see in a thriving coaching culture in a mental health care organization?**
>
> **On a good day:**
> Staff mindful of, and connecting with, the core purpose and values of the organization
> Staff routinely asking astute questions and communicating effectively
> Staff focusing on the achievement of relevant goals, being solution-focused and thinking flexibly
> Staff reflecting in a worthwhile way, with consequent benefits to the quality of their work and their own contentment
> Staff, including managers and leaders, giving and receiving feedback (including about tough truths)
> Staff involved in informal coaching and mentoring relationships
> Managers 'bossing about' less and coaching more; supporting the development and resourcefulness of the workforce
> Senior leaders walking the walk as well as talking the talk when it comes to coaching
> Staff trained and employed as internal coaches offering formal coaching sessions to other employees

Non-clinical coaching activity (by which I mean coaching activity focused within the mental health care workforce rather than with service users/carers directly) can take a number of forms. These include:

- informal coaching style conversations between colleagues
- formal coaching sessions provided by internal coaches
- managers using a coaching style of leadership/management

The first of these, informal coaching style conversations between colleagues, implies a routine style of communicating within the workforce that emphasizes a stance of curiosity, faith in each other's capability and a sense of unified purpose. The second aspect of a coaching culture, internal coaching, will be discussed in detail later in the chapter. A coaching management style involves looking for the best in people and supporting them to realize their strengths, rather than focusing heavily on weaknesses. Leaders with a coaching style allow staff the space to experiment more (within reason) and when mistakes happen, such leaders value learning over blame. That does not mean avoiding tough feedback; it means giving and receiving it in a considered way.

Leaders who seek to implement and sustain a coaching culture need to have clarity as to why and how they will do so. They should be mindful that this process requires significant investment of time and money, and, for the culture to thrive, the workforce needs to be on board and able to see some merit in the endeavour (van Niuewerburgh, 2015).

It follows that when workers feel valued and valuable in the context of an organization-wide coaching culture, they will probably be happier, more innovative and more productive. Other potential benefits might include improved staff self-awareness, better communication and smoother adjustment to organizational changes.

It can be difficult to demonstrate that the potential benefits outlined above are attributable to a flourishing coaching culture in an organization. For this reason, proper attention should be given to the evaluation of coaching within mental health service systems. For example, in the case of an internal coaching initiative, relevant questions include: What does an evaluation of internal coaching need to show and to whom? Will evaluation focus on qualitative or quantitative information? How will the value of coaching outcomes be estimated? To what extent will the impact of internal coaching for individuals tally with its effect at organizational level?

The consideration of such points is completely in keeping with the questions that coaches ask coachees every day about setting goals and measuring progress towards their attainment – that is, 'what outcome do you want?' and 'how will you know if you have got it?'

A Development Coaching Initiative for Psychiatrists (DCI)

The following summary outlines the intention, process and findings of an internal coaching initiative for psychiatrists employed in a NHS mental health organization in Northern England. This synopsis refers to the initial 30-month period of the initiative. For readers who are considering setting up in-house coaching arrangements, I hope that the information in the following paragraphs contains useful, practical elements. I do not present this as an academic write-up and I do not claim that the initiative was flawless. I offer this as an indicative report about a working initiative to give you food for thought.

Development Coaching Initiative: intention and background

I set up the Development Coaching Initiative for Psychiatrists in consultation with the medical leadership in the organization in which we work. Our aim was to promote the developmental aspects (both professional and personal) of the medical appraisal system for non-training grade psychiatrists.

As medical doctors, all psychiatrists are required to undergo a medical appraisal process. At their annual medical appraisal meeting, a psychiatrist presents evidence to their appraiser (usually a senior medical doctor who has received specific appraisal training) so that the latter:

- understands what the psychiatrist's work and job role involves
- can form an accurate impression about how well the psychiatrist is performing

- can consider with the psychiatrist the next steps for continued personal and professional development (Roy, 2012)

All three components of an appraisal meeting (listed above) lend themselves to coaching style conversations, particularly the last one (i.e. promoting development). However, it seemed that the emphasis at appraisal meetings tended to be on checking crucial information and documentation about the first two aspects. The developmental component of the appraisal process often took a back seat.

This relative relegation was understandable given that stringent and well-recorded appraisal of professional practice and performance is mandatory for professional revalidation by the General Medical Council (GMC), the regulating body for all medical doctors in the United Kingdom. In short, medical doctors cannot practise legitimately if they are not involved appropriately in a thorough appraisal process that inspects their work (GMC, 2013).

It was agreed that a direct indicator of success for this coaching initiative would be reports from the participating psychiatrists that the coaching was useful developmentally, along with appraisers' positive impressions. In addition to the potential developmental benefit that coaching conversations might provide to individual doctors, we also hoped for associated advantages in service provision. Finally, we believed that the Development Coaching Initiative could send an important message to the existing psychiatric workforce and potential recruits: that the organization's medical leaders cared about the ongoing progress and welfare of their psychiatrists.

Although I am here discussing the appraisal process for psychiatrists, the territory covered is also relevant to the appraisal systems of other staff groups in mental health care organizations. Coaching can have a similar role in supporting their appraisal schemes.

Development Coaching Initiative: the process

Almost two hundred non-training grade psychiatrists working in the organization were eligible to take up this appraisal-related coaching offer. Their participation was entirely voluntary.

When the initiative first started, psychiatrists were offered a single coaching session per appraisal year (i.e. the 12 months between annual appraisal meetings). Over time, however, it became apparent that some psychiatrists wanted more sessions, others were interested in trying 'one-offs', while some were unlikely to take up the invitation at all. Therefore, subsequently the offer was increased to a maximum of four sessions per appraisal year. Sessions were bookable on a 'one at a time' basis, rather than as a pre-scheduled block of meetings.

I provided the coaching. Psychiatrists were able to access another internal coach, separately from the Development Coaching Initiative, if preferred or more appropriate – for example, if an ethical issue meant I should not take the role of coach for someone. I will note here that ideally, internal coaching programmes should draw routinely on a pool of diverse internal coaches. (We will explore ethics and internal coaching more in the next chapter.)

In the following, I will outline basic details of the Development Coaching Initiative. First, I sent an email to the psychiatrists, informing them about the initiative and inviting them to enquire further or book a coaching session (see Box 16.2).

Box 16.2: Development Coaching Initiative: initial, brief email about the coaching offer

The Development Coaching Initiative for psychiatrists:
Coaching conversations – exploring and developing your professional and personal potential

Dear Colleagues,

Psychiatrists in our organization can now access up to four one-to-one coaching conversations per year* with a professional coach (who is also an experienced consultant psychiatrist).

Sessions are bookable flexibly, one at a time as required, rather than as a scheduled block.

Please email me directly for further information, or if you would like to arrange a coaching conversation.

*This initiative aims to make the annual appraisal cycle more developmental.

For those psychiatrists who were interested in participating, I then provided basic coaching contract information (see Box 16.3).

Box 16.3: Development Coaching Initiative: basic coaching contract information

The agenda of your session is your own to set.

Please consider what you would like to have as an outcome from our conversation.

Confidentiality

- Every conversation will remain confidential unless you disclose an illegal activity or there is a risk to yourself or to others.
- I may discuss with my coaching supervisor (independent of this organization) how we have worked together – in an anonymized way.
- For admin purposes, I keep a list of the psychiatrists who have accessed coaching conversations, with the dates. I do not keep records about the

content of coaching conversations, or pre-conversation information, after your coaching conversation has taken place.

- After each coaching conversation, I send you a brief email which may refer to the broad topic of our conversation, but contains no specific details.
- Key themes emerging from the Development Coaching Initiative may be put to the medical directorate leadership – with **no** individually identifiable information – for organizational learning.

Openness
- If I say or do anything that you do not feel comfortable with or if you have a concern with the way we have worked, please let me know. Any problems, please contact the Medical Director.

Feedback
- You have the opportunity to submit feedback via a brief online form of 4 short questions only.

Please confirm your agreement with the above. Please contact me with any questions or comments.

Thank you.

Once psychiatrists had booked their coaching conversations, they were sent a brief, optional, pre-conversation form to complete a week beforehand (see Box 16.4).

Box 16.4: Development Coaching Initiative: optional pre-conversation form

Dear Colleague,

If you would like to, please complete this brief form and return it by email before our coaching conversation.

Re. the statements below, please indicate the *two* main ways in which I may be most useful for you.

- Supporting me to clarify goals
- Supporting me to clarify plans
- Encouraging me to reflect constructively on what is important to me
- Supporting me to think constructively about my relationships with people at work
- Supporting me to distinguish between what I can and can't change
- Helping me to explore how I could change my behaviour
- Helping me to explore how I could change a problematic situation, assuming that it can be changed

- Supporting me to adjust to a problematic situation, assuming that it can't be changed
- Something else

You may also want to answer the following questions briefly:

1 What is the 'topic/issue' that is most important for us to focus on when we meet?
2 When we meet, what would you like to be the outcome of that coaching conversation?

THANK YOU FOR TAKING THE TIME TO DO THIS DATE

Note: This was based on a form developed by Windy Dryden and Jenny Forge, which appears in Dryden (2019).

The coaching sessions then took place, face-to-face or virtually, and typically lasted between 60 and 90 minutes. Conversations followed a CLEAR structure (see Chapter 5). Afterwards, coachees were invited to keep their own summary notes if they wished using the form shown in Box 16.5.

Box 16.5: Development Coaching Initiative: optional post-conversation form

Date

One key insight or reflection from the conversation
One key intention following from the conversation
When will I do this/act on my intention?

Coachees were also invited to re-book a further session at some future point, after a period of reflection and action in relation to what they had discussed and agreed in the coaching conversation. Finally, participants were requested to complete, anonymously, a short online feedback form of four questions as shown in Box 16.6.

Box 16.6: Development Coaching Initiative: online feedback form (anonymous)

Please indicate your response to the following statement (strongly disagree, disagree, neither agree nor disagree, agree, strongly agree):

The development coaching was useful.

In brief:

- What was most useful for you?
- What would have been more useful for you?
- Could you please possibly sum up your experience of the coaching in one word/phrase.

Thank you for taking the time to do this.

Development Coaching Initiative: findings

Over an initial, nearly two-and-a-half-year period, I undertook 236 formal, one-to-one coaching sessions with 70 non-training grade psychiatrists. With respect to the 53 per cent of coaching sessions for which recorded written feedback was obtained, the participating psychiatrists agreed that 100 per cent of the sessions were useful. Furthermore, this was deemed as strong agreement for 86 per cent of these sessions. It was notable the coaching offer was taken up to a proportionately greater extent by female psychiatrists.

I would like here to be in a position to quote some of the positive anonymous feedback received, but I did not seek permission from participants at the time and so it would not be ethically appropriate.

Psychiatrists perceived benefits of having dedicated personal sessions in which to reflect on their work, together with a coach who was supportive yet able to challenge them. They valued the opportunity to focus on their developmental hopes, goals and plans. They also used the coaching conversations to constructively explore a variety of subjects concerning their day-to-day working life such as team functioning and prioritizing workload.

A number of psychiatrists' appraisers reported their impression that the initiative made a positive contribution both to the professional development of psychiatrists, and overall support of the psychiatrist workforce. A senior appraiser wrote:

> This is an initiative that can help staff, colleagues and the organization significantly; in my view sustaining this effort will be very rewarding in terms of staff satisfaction thereby leading to improvement in quality and safety in terms of patient care.[2]

Following the initial period, the Development Coaching Initiative received approval to continue as an established initiative, with routine, ongoing review of its usefulness. Although not explicit objectives of the Initiative, two further apparent benefits to this programme were identified.

First, it seemed that the coaching possibly had a positive influence on retention of the psychiatrist workforce. This was welcome news. Throughout the UK, there are significant concerns about the recruitment and retention of psychiatrists and other mental health practitioners. Good professionals are precious and worth holding onto. Some Initiative coachees deliberated about leaving the organization, and even about quitting medicine altogether. Such psychiatrist coachees typically held particularly stressful jobs with complex responsibilities and dynamics. Some felt that their everyday work had become less connected to the key values and motivations that had inspired them to join the profession.

These psychiatrists used their coaching time to explore their current work situation from different perspectives, and as part of their personal bigger picture. Almost all these psychiatrist coachees concluded that there were actions they could take in their current post, or occasionally in a related role within the organization, to improve their professional situation. For example, a coachee who discussed the likelihood of leaving the organization, decided instead to follow a change plan that involved staying within the organization. That plan was consolidated during coaching. Almost a year on from our last coaching session, this psychiatrist emailed me to say:

> *Things are much, much better. I can't thank [the coaching] enough for helping me see the bigger picture at a difficult time ... Enjoying psychiatry again, having more time and mental space for my family.*[3]

Secondly, I believe this initiative helped to enhance the well-being of some psychiatrists who took up the offer of coaching. In these conversations, psychiatrists were able to explore how to manage the impact of their work on their health and vice versa. A number of coachees reported benefits to their well-being following the coaching. One psychiatrist wrote to me with the following observations:

> *[Coaching has] helped me to overcome some challenging situations in the work environment, and supported me to strengthen my resilience during a prolonged period of difficulties. [It has] enabled me to identify and achieve many short-term goals successfully, with very positive impact on both work and family life, while also keeping my longer term goals in sight.*[4]

For psychiatrists who participated in the Initiative during sick leave, coaching conversations helped them to remain connected with work and steadily return to it.

Having made a case in this chapter for the value of internal coaching initiatives in mental health care organizations, in the next chapter I take a deeper look at internal coaching. In particular, we will explore the important topics of ethics and supervision in the internal coaching context.

Notes

1   Conversation with Katharine St. John-Brooks, 1 May 2020.
2   Correspondence from a senior medical appraiser/consultant psychiatrist, with permission.

3 Correspondence from a consultant psychiatrist who participated in coaching, with permission.
4 Correspondence from a psychiatry specialty doctor who participated in coaching, with permission.

References

Dryden, W. (2019) *Single-Session Coaching and One-At-A-Time Coaching: Distinctive Features*. London: Routledge.

General Medical Council (GMC) (2013) *The Good Medical Practice Framework for Appraisal and Revalidation*. Manchester: GMC.

Parsloe, E. and Leedham, M. (2017) *Coaching and Mentoring: Practical Techniques for Developing Learning and Performance*, 3rd edition. London: Kogan Page.

Roy, D. (2012) Appraisal for psychiatrists, *CPD Online*. https://elearning.rcpsych.ac.uk/learningmodules/appraisalforpsychiatrists/introduction/moduleintroduction.aspx (accessed 4 June 2021).

St. John-Brooks, K. (2018) *Internal Coaching: The Inside Story*. London: Routledge.

van Nieuwerburgh, C. (ed.) (2015) *Coaching in Professional Contexts*. London: Sage.

17 Internal coaching matters

Introduction

As we saw in the previous chapter, internal coaching can make a difference in mental health care organizations. In this chapter, I argue that people planning and delivering internal coaching initiatives should think through potential pros, cons, risks and implications.[1] This chapter casts a spotlight on some necessary deliberations for would-be internal coaches. In particular, with respect to how they might choose the right course of action when there is a complex decision to be made.

The chapter is in three parts. The first of these is a long section which addresses the crucial yet bumpy territory of ethical dilemmas associated with coaching, and with internal coaching specifically. I include brief, fictional case examples to add flesh to the bones of ethical quandaries.

Next, I emphasize that coaching supervision should be part and parcel of any internal coaching programme, and offer key points about the nature of effective coaching supervision. The final section provides a case study involving an internal coach and a mental health practitioner (the latter worked in a community mental health team).

Ethical dilemmas

On the horns of an ethical dilemma is not a comfortable place to be. There are some behaviours that would be obviously unethical for a coach to get tangled up in. These include a coach gossiping with a coachee about another colleague, pressing a coachee for inappropriate inside information, or chatting with friends over coffee about someone's coaching sessions.

Other matters are less 'barn door' when it comes to choosing the right thing to do. Issues about confidentiality or boundaries are often at the root of ethical predicaments where there is no obvious right answer, and the facets of the situation need to be carefully weighed up (St. John-Brooks, 2018). With these tricky situations, and in the absence of easy solutions, the coach needs to stay self-aware and act professionally. They need to be true to the agreed coaching contract and remember precisely why they are meeting with the coachee.

Ethical dilemmas are likely to be thrown up more often when the internal coach and coachee work in the same part of the organization. When these tight spots occur, the coach will be thankful that:

- they went through a proper contracting process with the coachee at the outset (particularly about the remit of coaching and the limits of confidentiality)
- they have regular coaching supervision with a trusted coaching supervisor
- their training as a coach involved attention to a code of ethical conduct

As coaches, we need to be able to articulate our reasons for deciding on a particular course of action, or lack of action, in response to an ethical dilemma. It is useful to consider what respected peers would do in a similar situation, and to reflect on how we would feel about defending our decision in a formal investigation. What about if we were to read about it in, for example, the *Northern Echo*?

Sometimes, despite good intentions, we may make a wrong call. Inevitably, we will not make perfect decisions all of the time. When we have formed a poor judgement, it is best we acknowledge it, apologize as appropriate, do what we can to make amends, learn from it and then let it go. But I know that this can be much more easily said than done.

Let's now consider five areas where, typically, ethical issues can arise in internal coaching:

- coach loyalty to both the coachee and the organization
- shared colleagues
- internal coaching in relation to managers
- welfare concerns
- bullying concerns

Coach loyalty to both the coachee and the organization

When at their most effective, internal coaches have a clear remit for their coaching role and know where they fit in their organization's big coaching picture. They have a duty and a loyalty both to the coachee and to the organization. But balancing the two is not always straightforward.

It is to be expected that coachees will occasionally feel badly done to by employers, and may want to spend time in coaching conversations bitterly lambasting the organization. The complaints may have some justification. Yet coaches are right to stay mindful that they are hearing one side of the story, and should resist slipping blindly into a Drama Triangle (see Chapter 2) where the coach plays the rescuer role, the coachee is cast as distressed victim and the organization is seen as persecutor.

Internal coaches may come to a conclusion that they have a 'tough truth' to share with the coachee. Imagine that an internal coach gains the distinct impression by what Lizzy, a coachee, says, that Lizzy is probably not willing to pull her weight in a busy community mental health team. Lizzy wants to use coaching conversations to complain about the scrutiny that her work performance is under, and to explore ways to escape this scrutiny.

This is not a comfortable situation for the coach. Is it time for a robust challenge to Lizzy? Time to speak the tough truth as the coach sees it? Or is that straying way into the realms of inappropriate judgement about Lizzy's work? Or drifting into some form of totally misplaced performance management?

There are ways to make progress in such situations, especially if coach/coachee rapport is good. The coach should, as the Post Office labels say, 'Handle with Care', and take time to think things through based on the individual circumstances. The coach might voice their discomfort out loud to the coachee. Or the coach might suggest the coachee step into the metaphorical shoes of others involved.

Another ethical dilemma that can arise is when an employee comes to coaching wanting to, for instance, discuss how a problem in their marriage or family life is impacting upon their work. This type of conversation could easily become primarily about the personal problem and little about work.

Should an internal coach work with a coachee on whatever they feel they need, even if its link to their job seems tenuous? Say Rohan comes for coaching stating emphatically that the quality of his work improves greatly when he is in a good physical fitness routine. He wants to use the coaching sessions to work on his motivation and training plan for an upcoming marathon. He assures the coach that successful completion of that marathon will be a huge confidence boost, with an energizing effect on him professionally as a hospital ward manager.

What should the coach think about that? How would the organization's coaching lead view that if they were aware of it? This kind of question again highlights the need for the coach to contract clearly, and to access good coaching supervision to help with ethical questions. Such an area may or may not be within the remit of the internal coaching provision. Leaders and coaches within the organization need to have thought in advance to what extent these kinds of decisions are at the discretion of individual internal coaches.

Shared colleagues

The internal coach and their coachees are like horses sharing the same paddock. Sometimes, it can be useful that the coachee is aware the coach has knowledge of the organization from the inside. It also means that inevitably there will be times when the coaching conversation partners know the same people.

Generally in coaching conversations, it is unhelpful if talk becomes concentrated continuously on the actions or personality of someone other than the coachee. The coach should, of course, listen, but is wise to avoid getting drawn into a dialogue about people not present. Otherwise, the coaching process can be derailed. The coachee can be distracted from the task in hand, which in large part is to explore their own thinking and make plans about their own actions, not speculate about someone else's.

A coachee's focus on third parties can be particularly distracting for internal coaches (compared with external ones), because the coach will likely know some of the people the coachee mentions. The coach may have their own impressions and might struggle to remain objective. Internal coaches should exercise self-understanding and professionalism in such circumstances, and it is only fair that they are straight with the coachee about the shared acquaintance. If the coachee or coach is uncomfortable with that fact, the coachee may need to team up with an alternative coach.

I have let know people who have joined me for coaching conversations that I am on good terms with the person they are talking about, and it has not resulted in the discontinuation of the coaching. However, I have also made it clear to coachees that there are other internal coaches with whom they could meet instead. Trust, integrity and probity are meaningful words, not platitudes. The reputation of individual coaches and of internal coaching programmes stands or falls on these matters. It is worth remembering that a perceived breach of trust can be as damaging as an infringement that has actually occurred.

Internal coaching in relation to managers

As noted earlier, when I refer to internal coaches, I mean employees working specifically as trained coaches within the same organization that employs the coachees. I am *not* referring to managers who use a general coaching style of leadership with their workers (see Chapter 16). The latter are, of course, vital for a true coaching culture, but internal coaches should not manage the people for whom they provide designated coaching, or figure in their management hierarchy.

Internal coaches are sometimes asked by managers if certain employees are accessing coaching and/or about the content of those coaching conversations. Unless agreed in the terms of the organization's internal coaching programme and in the coaching contract process with the coachee, the coach should resist such requests from managers. While such requests may stem from a supportive intention on the part of the manager, they are likely to violate the confidentiality of the coachee. Managers usually respond graciously when coaches decline to divulge information about coaching conversations.

Welfare concerns

Another issue that arises on the ethical front is when the coach has concerns about the well-being and safety of coachees or others around them.

In mental health organizations, internal coaches may well also be mental health practitioners, say psychologists or psychiatrists. Of course, some of the skills that make them an effective mental health practitioner are valuable in their internal coach role. But when they coach colleagues, it is helpful if internal coaches keep their coach hat on and their mental health practitioner hat on the peg (see Chapter 11).

Stressed staff may reasonably seek internal coaching to help them better manage practical and emotional elements of work. Stress can tip into significant anxiety or lasting low mood, and it sometimes can be difficult to discern at what point that tipping has occurred. When a coachee is in extreme emotional distress, the coachee and coach may need to think together about involving additional supports, which might be family, the GP or employee psychology service (or equivalent).

What if the coachee is reluctant to involve anyone else but the coach is very concerned? The coach must weigh up the important principle of respecting the coachee's decision against other key considerations. Is the coachee's state of mental health putting themselves or others at risk? The coachee may be responsible for important clinical or service management decisions that they are not currently mentally in a good position to make. Or the coachee might be directly caring for dependent or vulnerable people.

Say, for example, a new coachee, Suzy, arrives late for a coaching conversation one morning. She has a senior role in Mental Health Service Development with considerable responsibility. She is looking a bit worse for wear, complaining of a hangover and possibly – the coach thinks – smelling slightly of stale alcohol. Suzy explains, 'We had quite a night at book club!' During the coaching session, Suzy says she has recently been finding it harder than ever before to keep on top of work.

The next coaching session takes place six weeks later. Suzy again arrives looking ragged and bleary eyed. 'I had a few drinks too many with an old friend last night', she says. Part way through the second coaching conversation, the coach asks for Suzy's permission to say what is on his mind. Suzy agrees, so the coach carefully tells her about his observations, and reflects back to her that she has begun both coaching conversations with a mention of alcohol. These comments are not received well. Suzy declares that she has not come to coaching for a lecture, and she ups and leaves the room. The coach sits there, feeling clumsy, listening to the sound of Suzy's angry footsteps receding down the corridor.

The coach considers what to do and decides not to act straightaway, but to sleep on it and discuss the situation with his coaching supervisor. The following morning, he receives an email from Suzy. In it, she apologizes for 'flying off the handle' and requests another meeting to help her think about 'sorting things out'. The coach agrees to a further session with a view to supporting Suzy to consider what she will do. But the coach anticipates that the 'sorting out' to which she refers will not fall entirely within the remit of the internal coaching programme, even if coaching may play a part.

Once again, this example points out the importance of a coach's awareness of the limitations of their role and competence. In extreme circumstances and when the coach is worried about a coachee's welfare, the coach may have no choice but to take their concerns outside the coaching room.

Bullying concerns

Coaches may face a situation where there appears to be evidence that a coachee or a colleague of the coachee is being bullied within the organizational hierarchy. The challenge for the coach and coachee together is to come up with a plan to properly address the problem. The problem gets stickier if, despite evidence of bullying and associated emotional distress, the coachee is clear they do not want the bully to be confronted. There is usually a way through to agreement on a satisfactory course of action. The key is that the coach listens well to the coachee, takes into account multiple perspectives, checks organizational policy and seeks specific advice, as necessary, in addition to their usual coaching supervision.

Suggestion for you

Consider what you would have done if you were an internal coach working with:

- Rohan (re. his running agenda?)
- Lizzy (re. not so busy?)
- Suzy (re. alcohol?)

The importance of coaching supervision

In mental health care organizations, it is well understood that mental health practitioners must receive regular clinical supervision in relation to their work with service users and families. Similarly, internal coaches must receive regular coaching supervision provided by properly trained supervisors, to support and inform their work with coachees.

As noted in Chapter 3, coaching supervision provides an opportunity for coaches to develop, feel supported, ensure quality and address difficulties.[2] Supervision may involve discussion of tools and techniques, but that is not usually the central part of the process. A coach's professional practice and decision-making are examined by the supervisor and coach in conversation together. The supervisor can help the coach to increase awareness of blind spots. This occurs through exploration of emotions and patterns occurring in the coach's work that would not be talked about elsewhere. A shared sense of psychological safety is key if supervision conversations are to be authentic and worthwhile.

The Henley Eight (Hawkins et al., 2019) is a set of eight questions put together by coach trainers at the Henley Centre for Coaching/Association for Coaching 'to guide self-reflection, enhance situation awareness and support personal development'. Specific areas of inquiry valuable in coaching supervision are listed in Box 17.1, paraphrased from The Henley Eight.

Box 17.1: Areas of inquiry in coaching supervision, paraphrased from 'The Henley Eight'

1 What the coach picked up on
2 How the coach responded in terms of their thoughts, feelings and actions
3 What the coach learnt about themself personally
4 What the coach learnt about themself as a coach
5 How that learning is valuable for the coach
6 What blocks might arise in their future coaching work
7 What emerged for the coach while considering the areas above
8 How the coach's practice might change as a result

It is a given that with coaching, as with mental health practice, there are times when we feel less effective in our role than we want to be and question the value of some of our work. In these circumstances, a supervisor's honest encouragement and support can make a restorative difference and offer constructive perspectives. And when a coach discusses in supervision a great piece of coaching work they have done, the supervisor can join them in registering and reinforcing this success.

While supervision is important in relation to all forms of coaching, the sorts of ethical dilemmas described in the first part of this chapter underscore that it is a vital component of any internal coaching set-up.

An internal coaching conversation: a case study

The following case example contains a blend of elements drawn from my experience of internal coaching work with mental health service colleagues. These colleagues come from a range of professional backgrounds, including nursing, psychiatry, psychology, administration and organizational development. This case study highlights a coaching theme about communication, in particular, that of managing difficult conversations at work.

Case study context

Marita is a senior clinician in an inner-city community mental health team. The team manager, Ash, is known for having an abrupt style and is often perceived by team members as lacking empathy about the pressures they are under. This has seemed more apparent recently. Ash sometimes chides team colleagues loudly in public, and has no qualms about engaging in so-called 'brisk banter'. Marita is only too aware that one person's idea of brisk banter is another person's idea of humiliation. Marita and her colleagues are not clear about how to make things better. Her team colleagues look to Marita for a way forward as she is a senior clinician in the team. Marita is mild mannered and not by nature a person to seek out confrontation. She feels under increasing pressure to do something. But should she take specific action? And if so, what and how?

C in this CLEAR conversation

Marita came for a coaching conversation with me. This was her first coaching session, and we did not know each other beforehand. We covered the formal contracting aspects such as confidentiality and the scope of our internal coaching arrangement.

I asked her what she wanted to think about during the conversation. Marita inhaled and made a wincing expression. She outlined the situation about the team described above, and finished off by saying, 'So I suppose the thing is to change Ash?'. Then she paused and smiled ruefully, realizing that trying 'to change Ash' would not be the most helpful focus for our conversation.

I asked her what she would like to achieve by the end of our conversation. Marita said she would like to have some clarity about her next steps in relation to the team's situation. Marita added that she knew that she could not force Ash to change and wanted to explore constructive options that would improve the outlook for the team. 'I've just been hoping for a while now that things will improve, but I've had my head in the sand really'.

I inquired how she would know that she had achieved the outcome she wanted from our conversation? Marita said she would write some action points down about what she would do over the coming weeks, so that she could feel more effective in this situation. Then she added, 'And if I'm honest, I want to get rid of this horrid feeling about work that's bogging me down'.

I checked with Marita how challenging she wanted me to be during the course of the conversation, and she said, smiling 'Go for it … but back off if I'm in floods of tears. I'm only half joking by the way'.

L and E in this CLEAR conversation

In the exploration phase of the conversation, I invited Marita to consider her thoughts, feelings and where she herself fitted within this larger issue. Within the flow of the conversation, I used some (but not all) of the brief questions listed in Box 17.2, aiming to support Marita's exploration, evoke greater clarity and foster her sense of resourcefulness.

Box 17.2: Coaching questions for Marita

What part of the situation most needs to be resolved?
What is the reason it needs to be resolved?
What will happen if it is not resolved?

What will happen if it is resolved?
What's the bigger picture?
What do you know to be true about the team?
What do you know to be true about Ash's job?
What do you know to be true about yourself in this situation?
What patterns do you notice in the team?
What are you avoiding?
What are you assuming?
What contribution do you make to the situation?
What could you possibly do to help resolve the situation?

Marita seemed to engage in an open and brave way with the conversation, facing some uncomfortable truths and emotions. At one or two points, as she spoke, I acknowledged briefly, out loud, my impression about her courage and receptivity. I did not make any elaborate challenges, as it felt sufficient for me to add just occasional phrases, such as 'Are you sure about that?', 'Is there something else important about that that you aren't saying aloud?'

The following emerged for Marita during the course of the listening and exploration stages of our CLEAR conversation, with very little input from me, other than inquiry and reflective summary.

- Marita started to see the 'team/Ash' situation in terms of a Drama Triangle dynamic (Karpman, 1968), with the team in the role of collective victim and Ash cast as persecutor. (Marita knew of the Drama Triangle prior to our conversation, but she had not thought of it previously in relation to the team. I did not suggest this parallel to her, it emerged for her spontaneously.)
- Marita was feeling awkward about the prospect of any form of encounter with Ash that risked escalation into a showdown. Marita felt worried that the team's respect and liking for her would diminish if her attempts to improve the situation backfired and made things worse.
- Marita realized that during team discussions when Ash was not present, team members bonded by talking about Ash's apparent awfulness. This served to reinforce the victim perception of the team.
- Marita saw that regarding this situation from the Drama Triangle point of view, it might be possible for the team to move to a situation more in line with a Winner's Triangle (Choy, 1990; see Chapter 2). The Winner's Triangle would entail team members coming up with different and more creative ways of responding (i.e. moving out of victim role, even though still feeling vulnerable). In addition, Marita would not take on the rescuer role, and Ash would not be regarded so firmly as a persecutor.
- At this stage of the coaching conversation (i.e. at the end of the nominal exploration stage in CLEAR), Marita commented that stepping back to look at this bigger picture was useful. She said that she felt less helpless and more in touch with her courage when she viewed the situation from her new perspective.

A and R in this CLEAR conversation

It was then time to consider action steps, and Marita moved on as follows.

Marita decided that at her next one-to-one meeting with Ash, she (i.e. Marita) would broach the subject of team perceptions about Ash's communication and style. This meeting was to happen the following week. Marita decided to send an email to Ash in advance to say that she would like to use the conversation to discuss things that had been on her mind about team functioning and relationships. Marita resolved to include in the email that she was raising these issues in the spirit of seeking to improve team performance and sense of getting along together.

Marita chose to firm up her plan as follows:

- She would write the email carefully and send it to Ash three days before the conversation.
- Before the meeting, she would deliberate about the most important thing she wanted to achieve in the discussion with Ash, and about how she (Marita) wanted to come across. She would consider in advance what questions she would like to ask Ash as well as what questions Ash might ask her.
- Marita decided to look on the internet and in the library for useful information about having difficult conversations, and make some notes for herself.
- Marita also said she would block off some time that had become available to her due to a cancelled meeting, to read up about the organization's policies about bullying.

We agreed not to schedule a further coaching conversation at that point, but Marita said that she would contact me after her conversation with Ash. A few days later, I received an email from Marita (see Box 17.3).

Box 17.3: Email from Marita

Hello

Thanks again for the coaching session on Tuesday. It got me thinking more clearly and I feel stronger than I thought I was.

Just in case you're interested, I did some reading and some thinking as planned, and here are ten top tips for difficult conversations.

I'll be in touch as agreed after the conversation. Speak soon, KR, Marita

1 Name the difficulty early on, and know it won't feel easy
2 Think: What's the most important outcome to achieve in this conversation
3 Think: What am I avoiding? And what am I assuming?
4 Convey I want things to get better, and look for a sense of common endeavour
5 Convey my thoughts about my own contribution to the difficulty
6 Use questions rather than statements (which may be heard as an attempt to control)

7 Say 'I feel' or 'I would like' rather than 'you're being' (which can sound provocative)

8 Keep 'connected' with my breathing, keep it steady

9 Give specific information or examples about the difficulty

10 Keep constructive and civil and brave[3]

Marita called me a fortnight after our coaching conversation. She reported that the conversation with Ash had been less stressful than she had anticipated. In addition, Marita had appreciated the opportunity to see things more from Ash's perspective. Ash had acknowledged that she had been managing the team in 'a more heavy-handed way' than she intended. She had told Marita, without going into details, that she was experiencing some personal stresses. Ash subsequently mentioned to Marita that she had decided to seek some coaching for herself. Marita felt that there had definitely been a 'bit of a shift' and that this might be the beginning of some important improvements.

Marita explained that since our coaching conversation, she had avoided any involvement in 'Ash bashing' conversations with team colleagues. She hoped that this might be having, as she put it, 'a subtle modelling influence' on others in the team. She also felt pleased not to be, in effect, throwing fuel on the fire of team dissension with Ash.

Marita said that although she had not handled everything perfectly, she had been quite impressed with herself during her one-to-one conversation with Ash. Marita had managed to put into action some of the 'top tips' from her list (in Box 17.3). Marita then suggested she book a further coaching session to help her think how to consolidate her productive role in relation to team dynamics.

Suggestion for you

Reflections ...

- Did anything surprise you about the coaching conversation with Marita?
- If you had been the coach, what would you have done differently?
- Did you come to judgments or make assumptions about Marita, Ash and the team? For example, had you assumed Ash was male or female?
- Marita was already familiar with the Drama Triangle and brought it into the conversation as she thought about the situation.

Do you think it would have been appropriate for the coach to outline the Drama Triangle model to a coachee who did not already know about it? Or would that be straying away from coaching into mentoring or teaching?

Part 4 has demonstrated some of the rewards and challenges of workforce coaching within mental health care organizations. We will now move on to the concluding chapter, drawing together some of the coaching threads discussed throughout the book.

Notes

1 *Internal Coaching: The Inside Story* (2018), by Katharine St. John-Brooks, is a valuable resource for internal coaches.
2 See Association for Coaching supervision guide: guide.https://cdn.ymaws.com/www. associationforcoaching.com/resource/resmgr/AC_Coaching_Supervision_Guid.pdf (accessed 21 July 2021).
3 There are many sources of tips for making difficult conversations more constructive, including the books by Susan Scott (2017) and Eric Barker (2017).

References

Barker, E. (2017) *Barking Up the Wrong Tree*. New York: HarperOne.
Choy, A. (1990) The Winner's Triangle, *Transactional Analysis Journal*, 20 (1): 40–46. https://doi.org/10.1177/036215379002000105.
Hawkins, P., Turner, E. and Passmore, J. (2019) *The Manifesto for Supervision*. Henley-on-Thames: Association for Coaching and Henley Business School.
Karpman, S.B. (1968) Fairy tales and script drama analysis, *Transactional Analysis Bulletin*, 7 (26): 39–43. https://karpmandramatriangle.com/pdf/DramaTriangle.pdf.
Scott, S. (2017) *Fierce Conversations: Achieving Success at Work and in Life, One Conversation at a Time*. London: Piatkus.
St. John-Brooks, K. (2018) *Internal Coaching: The Inside Story*. London: Routledge.

Conclusion

18 Coaching in mental health settings: moving forward with awareness

Introduction

Mental health care is everyone's business. Those of us working in and those of us accessing mental health services can work together to improve them. The use of coaching practices has a growing part to play in this improvement.

In many Western cultures, people tend increasingly to employ the language of mental illness to describe themselves. Professionals have also broadened the boundaries of mental disorder to include more psychological predicaments. The subject of mental health and mental ill health is part of everyday discourse.

At a macro level, an increased readiness to ascribe mental 'illness' can be problematic. If it becomes ordinary to label temporary human responses to life's adversities as mental illness, and if the people experiencing such responses see themselves as ill, this can be unhelpful for them. It can also mean that those who suffer from severe mental illness may not have the extent of their situation understood.[1] Practitioners can usefully adopt a flexible coaching stance to support many people who find themselves somewhere on the complex and shifting spectrum between emotional distress and severe mental illness.

In this environment, this book argues that coaching can be a routine part of our attempts to ease psychological suffering. Coaching is crucial because this approach backs people to live their lives in ways that mean most to them, and can help equip them to contribute to the world in line with their values and strengths. Effective coaching is an empowering process which promotes people's sense of responsibility for their own lives.

This book is a source of a substantial amount of realistic guidance about the mindset, skills and practice of coaching in mental health settings. In writing it, I drew on many years of working as a psychiatrist, and more recently, as a professional coach. I appreciate the potential rewards, challenges and limitations of coaching methods for both coaches and for coachees. For these reasons, I have faith that this book can be of authentic value to those working in our field and therefore indirectly to the people we serve.

This concluding chapter is set out in three parts. The first summarizes some of the messages from this book about coaching work with individuals addressing mental health issues and with members of the workforce in mental health service organizations.

Next, I reflect on the scope to develop coaching in other settings in support of mental health and well-being. Here, in brief, I consider schools, prisons and social care settings, where I believe coaching can bring gains in relation to emotional functioning and practical solution-focused thinking. Such projects are already underway in some areas.

I end with an invitation for you to consider what you will take away from this book and use in your own work. I do not claim that coaching methods will be appropriate and effective in all situations. I am not so much beating a big bass drum for coaching as tirelessly tapping a tom-tom for it. Undoubtedly, coaching approaches have a lot to offer, and we cannot afford to lose out on the potential opportunities they can bring in terms of better care for service users and improved working lives for staff.

Summing up

We have seen throughout this book that the use of a coaching style underlines the merit of listening well, of asking effective questions, of helping coachees to clarify their key values and strengths, and in supporting coachees to set relevant goals and explore ways to achieve them. These key elements pertain both in clinical and non-clinical mental health service contexts, and a wide range of conversations can be enhanced when coaching principles are used.

Such interactions may take many forms. They might be a conversation between a service user and a practitioner, a coaching style chat between two colleagues, formal coaching for an employee provided by an internal coach, or a mental health service manager using a coaching style of management.

Whether the person doing the coaching is a designated and qualified coach or not, and whether the coaching takes the shape of a formal session or a coaching style conversation, there are fundamentals in common. Those leading and working in mental health services should give attention to the supervision, monitoring and evaluation of any coaching endeavours they are involved with – even though this governance may not be straightforward.

People training to be mental health practitioners or being taught to take on non-clinical roles in mental health care settings, would profit both personally and professionally by learning and practising coaching attitudes and skills. They should start to acquire these at an early stage on their career paths.

Opportunities abound to make the most of conversations by using coaching methods. Traditionally, formal coaching has been offered in the form of multiple sessions. But single conversations can also have a powerful impact.[2] One-off meetings can be especially useful when the rapport between coachee and coach is strong. Such conversations, for example, can lead coachees to make significant and lasting realizations about themselves. And when a coachee wants to bring about a change in their life, great headway can be made in a single discussion if it enables the coachee succinctly to gain clarity about:

- the change they want to make
- why they want to make the change
- how they can make the change
- when they will make the change
- their willingness to accept personal responsibility for making the change

In summing up, Box 18.1 shows some key points about the four parts of the book.

Box 18.1: Some take-away messages

In **Part 1**, I emphasized that coaching is about supporting people to make the most of their potential, and involves facilitation not fixing. We should care about ensuring coaching principles play a part in the organization and provision of mental health support. People may be great clinicians, highly competent non-clinical employees or skilled managers in mental health care organizations. Yet, whatever their role, they can gain an edge in their work if they learn and practise how and when to use coaching skills appropriately.

In **Part 2**, the focus was on a wealth of practical coaching know-how including real listening, deft questioning, goal defining and action planning. We can use these skills very effectively within the conversational structure of the CLEAR model, which shapes progress through five stages: contracting, listening, exploring, action and review. Coaching techniques (such as ThinkOn® tools) are valuable, and they should be used in a flexible and fitting manner. Coaching tools should be used in such a way as to enhance the natural flow of coaching conversations.

Part 3 highlighted the use of coaching in clinical mental health care settings. The promotion of personal recovery (i.e. an individual process towards living a meaningful life) is an important aim for mental health services. This differs from the traditional emphasis on 'getting better' – that is, in plain terms, eliminating symptoms. The five personal recovery processes of CHIME – connectedness, hope, identity, meaning and empowerment – are natural foci for coaching conversations. Co-creation and co-production projects, whereby professionals and service users/families plan and deliver support services together, are fertile ground for the growth of effective coaching practices that can reap rewards.

Part 4 of the book showed how coaching can be key in the organizational functioning of mental health care services. This can bring benefit to individual members of the workforce, the organization and therefore ultimately the population we are here for.

Where to next?

There is worthwhile and undeniable scope for further development of coaching approaches in mental health settings.

So where do we go from here with coaching in mental health care? From my point of view, further embedding coaching competencies in the workforce's everyday ways of working will bring ongoing benefits. I am not referring to any blanket implementation of set, formulaic coaching techniques. Rather, I mean encouraging staff to adopt coaching stances in ways that are attuned and responsive to particular contexts. Alongside this, there is a place for formal internal coaching sessions for the employees in mental health care systems.

The phrase 'mental health settings' can be understood in broad terms: I will reflect here briefly on coaching and mental well-being in association with children's education, the criminal justice system and social care. There is a justifiable spotlight on children's and young people's well-being and mental health in schools (Cowburn and Blow, 2017). Efforts by school staff to promote resilience and social and emotional development should include thoughtful attention to coaching principles. For example, in terms of children's development and well-being, let's consider the value of learning about active listening, constructive reflection and solution-focused thinking. It stands to reason that there are rewards to be had if young people gain familiarity with coaching habits, and proceed to carry into adult life the ability to embrace a coaching mindset.[3]

The increased rate of mental health problems amongst those in contact with the criminal justice system is well known. In 2014 it was reported in a NICE (National Institute for Clinical Excellence) document that an estimated 76 per cent of female remand prisoners and 59 per cent of male remand prisoners had an anxiety disorder or depression. This compared with 16 per cent of the general population. Coaching Inside and Out (CIAO) is a social enterprise, charitable organization and it demonstrates how coaching can be valuable for prisoners' mental health (McGregor, 2015). CIAO offers coaching to women in prison, supporting them to generate hope and motivation, to connect with their emotional strength, and to examine possibilities and choices for their futures with fresh eyes.

Many of those employed in the fields of social work, social care and local government work day-to-day with people experiencing psychological and psychiatric difficulties. For example, looked-after children are four times more likely to experience mental health issues than their peers.[4] The social care workforce makes an important contribution to improving people's mental health by looking at the attendant social aspects and social solutions to psychological problems and distress (Allen et al., 2016). The use of coaching methods in social work enables social workers to prioritize a practice based on the growth and agency of family members they work with (OSS Network, 2019).

What will you do?

For all the positives I have discussed about coaching, it is certainly not a miraculous remedy for all the challenges entailed in providing good mental health care and managing services. I acknowledge that some people working in mental health contexts will be keener on coaching than others. Some will wonder what all the fuss is about because they seem to use a coaching style already, one that just evolved naturally.

Whatever your level of enthusiasm about the use of coaching in mental health settings (and I hope it is substantial), thank you for reading this book and for considering the extent to which coaching will feature in your future work. I have confidence that the book will be useful for you in some way.

In line with typical coaching practice, I shall ask you, 'What is one insight you have gained from reading this book, and what is one intention you have as a result of reading it?'

Coaching conversations can be a source of rich learning for those involved. As coachees (and as coaches too), we may come to understand ourselves better, and achieve more clarity about what we can gain from and offer to our world. Reasons to show more compassion to ourselves and others may emerge. In coaching conversations, we can think about what we will meet on the road ahead, prepare to greet it well and make worthwhile onward journeys.

Notes

1 For further relevant discussion, see Foulkes (2021).
2 Windy Dryden has written extensively about the process and potential of one-off coaching conversations. See, for example, his *Single-Session Coaching and One-At-A-Time Coaching* (2019).
3 For further reading about coaching in schools generally, you may be interested in writing by authors such as Andy Vass.
4 CAMHS – facts and figures. https://www.local.gov.uk/about/campaigns/bright-futures/bright-futures-camhs/child-and-adolescent-mental-health-and (accessed 26 June 2021).

References

Allen, R., Carr, S., Linde, K. et al. (2016) *Social Work for Better Mental Health: A Strategic Statement*. London: Department of Health. https://assets.publishing.service.gov.uk/government/uploads/system/uploads/attachment_data/file/495500/Strategic_statement_-_social_work_adult_mental_health_A.pdf (accessed 26 June 2021).
Cowburn, A. and Blow, M. (2017) *Wise Up: Prioritising Wellbeing in Schools*. London: YoungMinds.
Dryden, W. (2019) *Single-Session Coaching and One-At-A-Time Coaching: Distinctive Features*. London: Routledge.

Foulkes, L. (2021) *Losing Our Minds: What Mental Illness Really Is – and What It Isn't*. London: Vintage.

McGregor, C. (2015) *Coaching Behind Bars: Facing Challenges and Creating Hope in a Women's Prison*. Maidenhead: Open University Press.

National Institute for Health and Care Excellence (NICE) (2014) *Mental Health of Adults in Contact with the Criminal Justice System*, November 2014. https://www.nice.org.uk/guidance/ng66/documents/mental-health-of-adults-in-contact-with-the-criminal-justice-system-final-scope2 (accessed 26 June 2021).

OSS Network (2019) *From Transmission to Transformation: Use of coaching practices within statutory children's social work, One Stop Social*, 5 June. https://onestopsocial.co.uk/2019/06/05/from-transmission-to-transformation-use-of-coaching-practices-within-statutory-childrens-social-work-social-work- (accessed 26 June 2021).

Index

Page numbers in italics are figures; with 'n' are notes.